MW01242068

Sydney

WORLD-CLASS JEWEL

Sydney
WORLD-CLASS JEWEL

**URBAN
TAPESTRY
SERIES**

TOWERY
PUBLISHING, INC.

ART DIRECTION BY *Brian Groppe*

Contents

THE WORLD IS COMING TO SYDNEY. WE'RE ABOUT TO BE rediscovered. Again. It's something we're used to, though, and frankly it doesn't scare us too much. When you have an important city located on one of the most beautiful stretches of coastline in the world, you can expect the world to come calling now and again.

This time, the world is coming to participate in the grand spectacle of the 2000 Olympic Games. Sure, we're a bit apprehensive; we've got enough crowded streets and trains as it is. But we've grown so fast that the prospect of welcoming a half million or so more visitors to our city is something we know we can accommodate, and all in all, we're delighted about the whole affair.

The site of the 2000 Olympic Games alone tells you a lot about our resolve, our resourcefulness, and our tendency to keep working on things until we get them just right. The 1,900-acre Olympic Village has been built in Homebush Bay, an area nine miles west of central Sydney that has been, over the years, home to an Aboriginal fishing site, a racecourse, a salt mine, an armaments depot, and a dump. Despite the early concern of some environmentalists, the finished product is being hailed as a model of design and the very picture of an ecofriendly park. Wetlands have been maintained, thousands of native trees have been planted, and a host of natural wildlife—including rare birds and amphibians—have been relocated to the area. What was once a forgotten corner of suburban Sydney is now poised to welcome the world to brand-new Olympic venues like the SuperDome, Olympic Stadium, and Aquatic Centre, all of which are an easy stroll from one another. And once the Games— which are to be held in late September—are over, Sydneysiders will

continue to enjoy the site when it becomes Millennium Parklands, the city's largest metropolitan park, quite a feat in a place known for its sprawling and magnificent spaces. Athletes' Village (solar powered, mind you) will become a housing complex.

All of the attention the Games will bring will help the billions of expected TV viewers around the world relearn what Sydney really is: one of the world's great metropolises. Sure, it's got its share of rather amazing history, despite its relative youth. And, it's a place that has retained its distinctive character. But what the world continues to learn, and relearn, is that Sydney is best regarded not as a provincial outpost "down under," but as an important centre for

commerce, tourism, culture, sports, and—lest we forget the nearly 4 million inhabitants—a place for making a life for yourself.

Part of what makes all of this grandness remarkable is that almost all of us are relative newcomers here. Unless you're a descendant of one of the Aboriginal peoples who have lived here for thousands of years, you tend to count your lineage in Sydney in terms of generations that usually don't extend beyond the "great-" stage. Great-grandfather, great-aunt, that sort of thing. Sydney's explosive growth, and its rise to prominence as an international community, has come fairly recently. That's why we're disposed to having such a sanguine attitude about visitors, even when they come in throngs and hordes, as they will this year for the Games.

As the excitement over the coming of the world builds, we grow more reflective. More anxious to show off our charms. And, most of all, more appreciative of the wonderful city we call home.

$\mathcal{I}$F YOU WANT TO GET A GOOD LOOK AT SYDNEY'S HARBOUR— past, present, and future all mingled into one grand vista—you can do no better than to trek up to Mrs. Macquarie's Chair. This is by no means the only grand vista to be had in Sydney, a city of breathtaking sights and stunning natural beauty. But it's as good as any and better than most. Here, a seat—carved into the rock moved to create a roadway along one of the points that jut into Sydney Harbour—affords a splendid view of the Sydney Opera House and the Harbour Bridge.

Mrs Elizabeth Macquarie, you should know, was the wife of Governor Lachlan Macquarie, who held office in the early 19th cen-

tury and helped transform New South Wales from strictly a penal colony to a free society. Mrs Macquarie concerned herself with slightly less radical issues, but she still needed the solace provided by constitutionals along a roadway being built in the Royal Botanic Gardens. When the convict labourers building the road saw her repeatedly pausing to take a breather at the same spot on a marvelous spit of land between Woolloomooloo Bay and Farm Cove, legend has it that they devised the rock chair in deference to the wife of a man they respected for his progressive views toward them.

Little did Mrs Macquarie know, when she delicately settled her bustle on the perch that had been carved for her, that a scant 200 years later, the harbour and foreshore of this provincial outpost known as Sydney would be teeming with such life. From here, you get an instant sense of both how and why Sydney has taken an

already beautiful harbour and actually improved upon it as it developed and grew. Here, before you, are a good many of the landmarks that the world commonly uses when it identifies Sydney as the city it is.

Such as . . .

The Sydney Opera House. An obvious visual benchmark, maybe, but a stunning one nonetheless. After considering a number of plans in the mid-1950s, the city accepted Danish architect Joern Utzon's majestic design—with a roof billowing like concentric sails. The only trouble was that it proved extremely difficult to actually erect the soaring walls and roof. Still, the design was so stunning that engi-

neers found a way to make it work. After 14 years of construction, the Sydney Opera House officially opened in 1973, and quickly became one of the world's distinctive urban landmarks. Today, the Opera House is a comprehensive arts complex, with dramatic productions, films, concerts, and (yes) opera performances, as well as four restaurants and cafés.

Or, another landmark, the Sydney Harbour Bridge. The bridge—called "the old coathanger" by tourists, much to Sydneysiders' disdain—was completed in 1932, and remains one of the world's longest arch-supported bridges. Climb the Argyle Stairs through an archway into the southeast pylon of the bridge. There are 200 stairs in all, but if you've got the legs for them, they'll lead you to a lookout with a spectacular view of the harbour. In addition to its beauty, the Harbour Bridge allowed Sydney's somewhat cramped business and government district to expand to the north shore. Today, North Sydney's commercial and residential area is coming to rival that of Sydney proper.

Or, more landmarks, like Circular Quay and The Rocks, which comprise the waterfront section where Sydney was born. Here, the big passenger liners from around the world tie up, and the city's transport systems come together. These areas have undergone considerable restoration and refurbishment of late, thanks to a rising awareness of their historical importance, but in many instances they retain the Victorian character of their original architecture. Today, they are popular areas for tourism, dining, nightlife, and commerce.

Inland a bit, there's Hyde Park, which dates back to 1792, when the colony's first governor declared it to be a public space. It was first used for racing and sporting—cricket, mainly—but in 1810, was

made into a formal park with gardens and walkways. Here, you'll find a number of statues and memorials, none more treasured than the ANZAC War Memorial that honors those service members who served and died in combat. (ANZAC, by the way, stands for Australian and New Zealand Army Corps.) The memorial is also noteworthy as a fine example of early-1930s Art Deco styling and architecture.

And, of course, there's the Royal Botanic Gardens, located between the Opera House and Mrs Macquarie's Point. The Botanic Gardens features acres of parkland at a site that Aborigines once favored as a fishing location, and where the first attempts at farming were made by European colonists (hence the name of Farm Cove, which forms one of the boundaries for the gardens). And it's here, not long after the Botanic Gardens was established in 1816, that Elizabeth Macquarie was honoured with the stone chair upon which she could sit and watch the big ships unfurl their sails against the amazing beauty of the harbour and the sky—and easily imagine that she was in paradise.

*I*F IT SEEMS THAT MUCH OF THE DISCUSSION, THUS FAR, HAS dealt with the past, the reason is simple enough: Sydney is a young enough city that the past is not quickly forgotten, yet it's old and cosmopolitan enough that the past is becoming a cherished commodity. In the midst of screaming modernity, the origins of the city—and, by extension, of all of Australia—reside right here in a small area of Sydney. Knowing just a bit about the origins of the city will help make sense of what seems, to residents, newcomers, and visitors all, like an obsession with things historical.

For all intents and purposes, the location of Sydney was something of a happy accident. The First Fleet, sailing under the banner

of Captain Arthur Phillip, reached the area in January 1788, landing first at Botany Bay, which Captain Cook had discovered 18 years earlier and where he had claimed Australia as a British crown possession. Phillip wasn't thrilled with Botany Bay, and continued searching for better anchorage. Just to the north, he located Port Jackson, and was immediately impressed. In a famous dispatch to Lord Thomas Townshend Sydney, the British Home Secretary, Captain Phillip described the splendid harbour at Port Jackson as "the finest harbour in the world, in which a thousand sail of the line may ride in the most perfect security."

With such grand pronouncement, Phillip anchored at an inlet he christened Sydney Cove (good relations with the Home Secretary no doubt in mind). It was here that the colony of New South Wales and the city of Sydney became a going concern.

Phillip's mission was, however, not one normally associated with locating beautiful places to drop anchor. His 11 ships carried some 750 convicts from England's overflowing prisons. Today, there's a certain left-handed social cachet associated with being a direct descendant of one of these original convicts. Following the first 750 would be another 150,000 people who had been convicted of what were sometimes exceedingly trivial crimes.

Rather than finding bliss, early Sydney dwellers—which is to say, either convicts or members of the British garrison, a corrupt bunch popularly known as the Rum Corps—had a hard time of it. The soil near Farm Cove was not (despite the name) good for growing much.

Better land was found inland a bit, but it had to be cleared by hand. Only years later did the newcomers cross the Blue Mountains and find good, arable land.

There were free settlers, too, who came to take advantage of cheap land and free convict labour that the government provided them. They propelled the trade—in, for instance, wool—that made the city grow quickly from a penal colony, which is most often and most kindly described as grim, into a proper mercantile center.

Another factor in Sydney's rise to glory was the arrival of the aforementioned progressive governor—Lachlan Macquarie—in 1810. During his 11-year tenure, Sydney came to resemble a quite presentable town. Macquarie, a Scot who had (for the time) some radical ideas about freedom and prosperity, instituted a program of building that resulted in hospitals, suitable army barracks, schools, government buildings, and parks like the Royal Botanic Gardens.

Still, the area remained a penal colony during its early decades, and a few of the early important personages were, themselves, doing

time. The most famous of the lot was Francis Greenway, an architect who had been sent to Australia to serve a 14-year sentence as a convicted forger. In Sydney, he built some 40 outstanding buildings, including St James Church and the Hyde Park Barracks for convicts. Under Macquarie's patronage, Greenway received a full pardon in 1819. His portrait graced the $10 banknote until recently, an ironic tribute to a man remembered—partly, at least—as a forger.

Lest we become too focused on the Eurocentric point of view, it needs to be stressed that the area we know as Sydney was a popular fishing and camping locale for Aborigines. They were not, it's safe to say, always happy to see the hordes of British settlers and con-

victs. Not only were they dispossessed of land they had known as their own, but many were wiped out by common European diseases, like measles and chickenpox, to which they had no immunity. Today, the descendants of tribes that once lived here mostly dwell in Sydney suburbs La Perouse and Redfern; few of them are what you would call thriving.

As was the case in almost all of Britain's other colonial excursions, Australia's Aborigines did little to stop the growth of European migration. Sydney grew by leaps and bounds as its trade routes opened with the rest of the world, and as industries such as the wool trade were developed. Between 1850 and 1890, the population of Sydney increased from 60,000 to 400,000. Suburbs sprang up—after

all, the main business and government centre is contained in a relatively small area of just five square miles—and Sydney's sprawl became the order of the day.

Throughout the 20th century, Sydney continued this manner of growth, becoming an international centre for commerce, manufacturing, governance, shopping and entertainment, tourism, shipping and transportation, and financial services. With a population of some 3.7 million, Sydney shares a good many characteristics with other great cities. It has a cosmopolitan mix of cultures and races, with Asian populations being well represented. Indeed, many swear that to have the best Chinese food in the world, you don't go to

China, you go to Sydney. (The same can be said for just about any cuisine, from Italian to Lebanese to Thai—as a city of fairly recent immigrants, Sydney has an amazing array of fine restaurants appealing to just about any taste.)

Such size and sophistication have a downside, of course. Sydneysiders bemoan the traffic, the congestion, the long commuting times, the occasional pollution—the same bellyaches that residents in other large metropolises share. But, on the whole, there are few who would trade the delicate and beautiful relationship between land and water, sun and sky that we love and cherish. Sydney may be big and noisy and fast paced, but its unique pleasures more than compensate for any problems that its rise to prominence has bred.

*S*YDNEY IS NUTS ABOUT SPORTS. SOME PEOPLE BRISTLE WHEN they hear this claim, but nobody disputes it, and most Sydneysiders are proud of their sporting heritage. From tennis and golf to cricket and football to all manner of water sports, Sydney knows how to enjoy itself. So many top tennis players hail from the area that it would be futile to list them. Horse racing has long been a favourite pastime; the city is home to four major racetracks, including the famous Royal Randwick.

Water sports are an obvious attraction in this city that seems to be made up of bays and beaches. In addition to Sydney Harbour, Greater Sydney incorporates two other substantial bays (Pittwater

and Botany Bay), and those who live here enjoy yachting and sailing like no place else in the world. Terrific beaches—some 30 of them—offer sun and sand for surfers, bathers, fishermen, and tan seekers. Since some beaches are obviously better suited for specific activities, visitors are advised to find a good guidebook to help locate just the right spot for just about any seaside activity.

As the Sydney Opera House symbolizes, the city is also a cultural centre of some magnitude. Symphony concerts, opera, ballet, modern dance, plays, pop music—there's plenty going on both at the Opera House and at a number of smaller theatres around town, and most of it is world-class and first-rate. The city's cultural and intellectual profile is heightened by the presence of a number of outstanding educational institutions, including the University of Sydney, the University of New South Wales, and Macquarie University.

Other attractions are equally fitting for a city of Sydney's stature. The Taronga Zoo is a proud addition for any city. Its natural habitat setting provides a fine home for the koalas that everyone, no matter

how jaded, must love. Sydney is sandwiched between two huge and magnificent national parks, a distinction shared by no other city in the world. Ku-ring-gai Chase National Park, located north of metropolitan Sydney, is home to a number of Aboriginal rock carvings and paintings, a place where carefully planned trails lead through an almost mystical environment. South of metro Sydney is Royal National Park, a favourite place for picnics and day trips.

And soon enough, the maps and guidebooks will have to include Millennium Parklands in this mix. The current home of the 2000 Olympic Games, this park will feature a number of outstanding sporting venues (needless to say), as well as a restored parkland, at

Homebush Bay. We expect crowds long after the 2000 Games are history.

The people of Sydney are taking this latest development in stride. Well, not exactly. Truth is, the coming of the Olympics is causing an enormous stir of excitement throughout the city, as Sydney prepares to welcome the world, and the world prepares to discover—again—what a great place this is.

*I*NSPIRED BY THE LIGHT AND energy of their native Sydney, artists Ken Done and Charles Blackman garner international acclaim through their diverse styles of painting.

THE STATELY MASTS AND SAILS OF schooners passing through Sydney Harbour are a study in efficient motion. Miniature models duplicate the larger ships perfectly, with one major omission: they have no crew.

A FITTING TRIBUTE TO ITS WATER-
front location overlooking Sydney
Harbour, the imposing rooftop
of massive Sydney Opera House
mimics the sweeping canvas sails
of passing ships. Covering 1.8 hectares, the facility was completed in
1973.

ᴅᴇsɪɢɴᴇᴅ ʙʏ ᴀʀᴄʜɪᴛᴇᴄᴛ Jᴏᴇʀɴ Utzon, the Sydney Opera House hosts around 3,000 events each year, attracting some 2 million people.

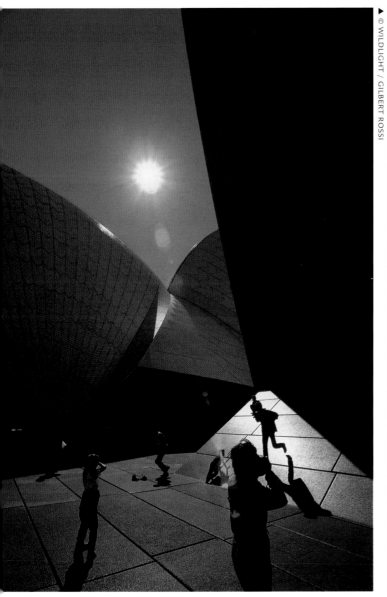

THE ORIGINAL DESIGN OF THE Sydney Opera House proved to be so complex that the facility took 14 years to build. After countless modifications, the result is an architectural marvel of organic shapes and patterns.

High atop the Sydney Harbour Bridge, "arch walkers" get an amazing view of the skyline. Daredevils can climb the entire span of the 50-storey arch, with the help of safety harnesses and handrails. The view from the Sydney Opera House proves equally enticing (bottom).

On a bright, warm day, Sydney's many waterways offer an array of aquatic activities, including sailing and surfing.

COMPLETED IN 1932 AND AFFEC-
tionately known as the Coathanger, the Sydney Harbour
Bridge connects the residential
area of north Sydney to the south
side City Centre.

An engineering novelty at the time of its opening, the Sydney Harbour Bridge's steel beams are secured by 36-metre-long anchoring tunnels dug into rock at each end. Functional as well as beautiful, the bridge supports the weight of some 200,000 vehicles daily.

𝓕OR MORE THAN A CENTURY, ferries have carried tourists and commuters to various locations throughout the Sydney area, from Darling Harbour to Watsons Bay.

THE HECTIC PACE OF COMMUTERS and workers has long dominated the streets of Sydney's business districts.

STRETCHING FROM GEORGE STREET to Macquarie Street, Martin Place plaza, opened in 1891, is a popular gathering spot for the lunchtime crowds of the City Centre.

COMPLETED IN 1995, THE MUSEUM of Sydney tells the story of the city from its first inhabitants to the eventual arrival of the Europeans (OPPOSITE). Itself a symbol of the past, the Australian Coat of Arms greets passersby from the doorway of the Law Court building on Macquarie Street (LEFT).

AUSTRALIA

OXLEY

DR LEICHHARDT

MACQUARIE S!

JUSTICE

WISDOM

THE BUILDINGS OF SYDNEY'S CITY Centre reflect a variety of architectural influences, from the classically Victorian Queen Victoria Building (OPPOSITE TOP) to the Art Deco Anzac Memorial in Hyde Park (THIS PAGE). A shopping centre of the grandest scale, the Queen Victoria Building—better known as the QVB—is guarded by a statue of the queen herself.

VICTO

THE GRAND SHOPPING ARCADES of Victorian Sydney have been carefully preserved in the Strand, a 100-plus-year-old building laden with boutiques and specialty shops (BOTTOM LEFT). Another treasure from the past, the Queen Victoria Building, underwent an overhaul in 1986, transforming the old produce market into what designer Pierre Cardin calls "the most beautiful shopping centre in the world."

© JAMES LEMASS

FROM THE CLOCK TOWERS OF THE
Sydney Town Hall (TOP LEFT) and
the Central Railway Station (TOP
RIGHT) to the orbicular windows
of St. Mary's Cathedral (BOTTOM)
and the Great Synagogue (OPPO-
SITE), the architecture of Sydney
reflects the city's old-world heritage.

The ornate decors of Sydney's historic halls and churches are fitting companions to the events that take place within their walls.

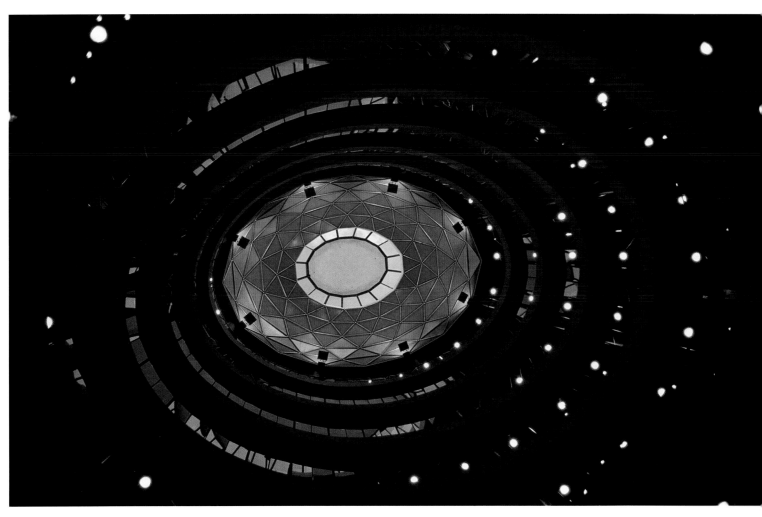

WHETHER FROM THE TOP DOWN or the bottom up, the helical staircase of the Garvan Institute of Medical Research is a dizzying proposition (OPPOSITE). Less spiral, though no less dramatic, are the cantilevered steps of the Elizabeth Bay House, a Greek Revival masterpiece.

VISIBLE FROM ALMOST ANYWHERE in the city, the AMP Tower offers visitors a bird's-eye view of their surroundings, sometimes to a distance of 85 kilometres. The tower's turret features nine levels that hold a coffee shop, an observation deck, and two revolving restaurants.

The observation floor of the AMP Tower (TOP RIGHT) provides a scenic view of Sydney, but it's all business for the watchful eyes focused on the city's financial future.

DARE
TO
KNOW

the art and science of Pacific voyages

A free exhibition until 29 November 1998

Sponsored by

 Sydney Mechanics'
School of Arts

 STATE LIBRARY OF
NEW SOUTH WALES

Occupying 30 hectares in the heart of the city, the Royal Botanic Gardens Sydney offers a quiet sanctuary from the bustle of daily life. Established in 1816, the site is a veritable living museum of native Australian plants, some species dating from 1770.

A NEW HEAVEN AND A NEW earth!" is how Henry Kingsley described the majesty of Australia. The shapes and colours evident in the country's flora and fauna are embodied in the waratah (TOP LEFT), the floral emblem of New South Wales.

FROM THE PROUD AND STATELY peacock to the laughing kookaburra, the feathered friends of Australia comprise a flock of their own.

▲ © WILDLIGHT / CLAVER CARRCLL

ONCE THE OFFICIAL RESIDENCE OF
the governor of New South Wales,
Government House overlooks
Sydney Harbour from its idyllic
location inside the Royal Botanic
Gardens Sydney.

Located in the City Centre, the Australian Museum (BOTTOM RIGHT) exhibits the archaeological origins of the area. But for a peek into Sydney's cultural and architectural beginnings, visit the Art Gallery of New South Wales (TOP AND BOTTOM LEFT) or historic Sydney Hospital, featuring *Il Porcellino*—a replica of a 17th-century fountain in Florence, Italy (TOP RIGHT).

Before the Europeans arrived, Sydney belonged to the Aborigines. Today, their heritage and customs—such as the didjeridoo, a wooden wind instrument—are kept alive through celebration and reflection, as in the works of acclaimed actor, director, and playwright Bob Maza (TOP RIGHT).

© WILDLIGHT / ANDREW RANKIN

ℱ ROM MEMBERS OF THE RUSSIAN Orthodox community to Hare Krishnas, from Buddhists to Muslims, people of all faiths can find a place to worship in Sydney.

A TRULY COSMOPOLITAN SOCIETY, Sydney boasts an extraordinary variety of cultures. Celebrations such as the Chinese New Year and the Matsuri Fiesta, as well as dancers in traditional Spanish garments, accentuate and define the city's eclectic heritage.

LOCATED IN THE CENTRE OF SYD-
ney's bustling Darling Harbour
area, the Chinese Garden provides
a portal to a quiet, serene world.
Also known as the Garden of
Friendship, its design was a gift to
Sydney from its Chinese sister city
Guangzhou, in the province of
Guangdong.

THE BLENDING OF CUSTOMS EN-
hances the flavour and variety of
Sydney's culinary treats. Shops and
markets citywide display a variety
of meats and breads, destined for
enthusiastic consumption.

THE CELEBRATION OF LIFE MANIfests itself in many ways, perhaps none so enjoyable as the face of a child.

Jubilation abounds for Sydney youth, expressed in the gleeful frolic of outdoor activities from dance to bagpipes.

Hᴇᴀʀ ʏᴇ, ʜᴇᴀʀ ʏᴇ: Fʀᴏᴍ ᴛʜᴇ town crier to the Royal Tongan Police Band (ʙᴏᴛᴛᴏᴍ ʟᴇғᴛ), Sydneysiders and visitors alike know how to dress for any official occasion.

A BUSTLING PORT CITY, SYDNEY welcomes ships of all sizes to dock. The 1940s luxury liner *Orcades* (OPPOSITE BOTTOM) helped pave the way for the modern *Queen Elizabeth II* (OPPOSITE TOP) and the American battleship USS *Independence* (TOP).

WITH MODERN TECHNOLOGY comes a price. Sydney's highly touted Collins-class submarine (OPPOSITE) has come under fire in a swirl of questions about its true capabilities. And, plans to add a second nuclear reactor at Lucas Heights—home to Australia's only such facility—have met with considerable citizen disapproval.

© JAMES D. SCHERLIS

To celebrate the landing of the First Fleet on January 26, 1788, Sydneysiders drop everything and head to Darling Harbour. Known plays of fireworks that appear over the water. Not to be outdone, Mother Nature illuminates the sky over the opera house with her own

THE EXTREMELY HIGH TEMPERA-
tures of the Australian summer
can ignite massively destructive
fires, but Sydney has an impressive
network of professionals and volunteers working round the clock
to protect both lives and property.

ONE OF THE LARGEST CITIES IN
the world, Sydney offers plenty of
room to roam. From ambulance
crews to those out on the town,
travel around the city is facilitated
by a system of freeways and
Metroads.

NOTHING BRIGHTENS THE NIGHT sky more than the neon signs advertising casinos and other forms of entertainment. From the old outback game of two-up to the more contemporary pokies, Australians enjoy a good wager.

RAGING INTO THE WEE HOURS OF the morning, Sydney loves a good beat. Whether in a rock concert or a nightclub, the city consistently draws the biggest names in contemporary music. Of course, Australia has been known to export a few big names as well, including Olivia Newton-John, INXS, and the Bee Gees.

THE COLOURFUL PLUMAGE OF
Australia is celebrated on the
streets of Sydney. From the West

are hardly a subdued lot. In fact,
the annual Gay and Lesbian Mardi
Gras is Australia's highest-earning

THE RELAXED ENVIRONMENT OF
Sydney flourishes with artists and
visionaries. Both Mark Seymour
(OPPOSITE), lead singer for the
Hunters & Collectors, and

New York-born architect George
Freedman have found in Sydney
the inspiration for a lifetime of
achievement.

WITH A MIXTURE OF COMEDIC talent, improvisational skills, and some nice weather, buskers keep pedestrians on their toes. A time-honored tradition, these street performers can be found in a variety of clever costumes. Terence Measham (THIS PAGE), director of the Powerhouse Museum, expresses himself in a slightly more subtle way.

FASHIONED AFTER CONEY ISLAND, Sydney's Luna Park has been a fixture on the amusement scene since 1935. Builder Ted Hopkins' creation features a giant face for an entrance and contains several buildings protected by heritage listing.

Sydney is a city of many faces, some made up and others simply serendipitous.

𝒯ILM-MAKERS GILLIAN ARMSTRONG (OPPOSITE) and Phil Avalon (TOP LEFT); writer Tom Keneally (BOTTOM LEFT); political satirists David Mouldfield and Paul Ian Hand- some Handpuppet (BOTTOM RIGHT); and comedian Mr P P (TOP RIGHT) demonstrate the wide variety of talent Australians enjoy.

Aᴴᵀᴱᴿ ɢʀᴀᴅᴜᴀʟʟʏ ꜰᴀʟʟɪɴɢ ɪɴᴛᴏ a state of ruin, Darling Harbour underwent a complete renovation, reopening in 1988, and now boasts

ture. Having transformed into something of a theme park, the harbour's plethora of attractions holds excitement for just about

Among the colourful sights found in Darling Harbour is the Sydney Aquarium (OPPOSITE TOP), home to two underwater viewing tunnels. At the heart of the harbour is the Sydney Convention and Exhibition Centre with its novel, circular fountain (OPPOSITE BOTTOM).

Whether you're looking out from the shores of Darling Harbour (OPPOSITE), from the breezy bow of a sailboat, or from high in the skies, the waters of Sydney glisten on a sunny day.

I LOVE HER FAR HORIZONS, I LOVE
her jewel sea," writes poet Dorothea
Mackellar about her beloved Australia. Sunbathers appear in droves
at these beaches, wearing little or—
in the case of Lady Bay (RIGHT)—
nothing at all.

THE OCEAN CAN BE A FICKLE friend to water enthusiasts, as the crashing post-storm waves of Coogee demonstrate (BOTTOM).

WITH LITTLE THOUGHT FOR THEIR own safety, the heroes of the surf aid and rescue those in trouble. At the pinnacle of physical fitness, lifesavers regularly challenge themselves and each other in surf carnivals—competitions with events based on the skills necessary to save lives.

Bondi Beach ranks among the world's best-known sites for sun-bathing, water sports, and even dining at one of its trendy cafes.

AGAINST A BACKDROP OF CRASH-
ing surf and brilliant skies, Sydney's
younger generation finds a place
to sprout wings—though some still
like to stick close to mom.

Near the Bondi Baths (oppo-site) is the headquarters of the Bondi Icebergs (LEFT). Founded in 1929, the organization requires potential members to swim three of four Sundays per month from May to September for a total of 75 swims in five years. On the first swim in May, the Icebergs drop blocks of ice into the water in order get the temperature just right—quite a different philosophy from that of the woolen-clad supervisor of a local cold-storage facility (RIGHT).

CONTINUALLY TESTING THEIR prowess, Australian athletes push themselves beyond the limit in events including the Sydney Half Marathon (OPPOSITE TOP), the men's Triathlon World Cup (TOP), and the women's Triathlon World Cup (BOTTOM). Sydneysider Chris McCormack (OPPOSITE BOTTOM) was the winner of the 1997 World Cup.

As host of the 2000 Olympic Games, Sydney is preparing to meet and compete with the best in the world. Second only to the United States in number of Olympic swimming medals, Australian athletes such as teenage phenom Ian Thorpe (OPPOSITE BOTTOM) are making their mark in the field.

The Sydney Swans, the local Australian Rules football team, draws scores of supporting fans to games at Sydney Cricket Ground (BOTTOM RIGHT). Sydney Football Stadium plays host to both Rugby League and Rugby Union games, not to mention one large rooster. It can also be the setting for some beautiful works of nature.

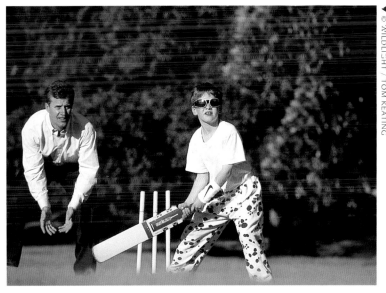

ℱROM CRICKET TO RUGBY TO FETCH,
Australians of all walks of life
enjoy a good game of ball.

S Y D N E

LAWN BOWLS AND BOWLS CLUBS are part of nearly every Sydney community. Even the statuary seems ready to join in the action.

It's all in the numbers. Whether wagering on a neck-and-neck horse race or packing into events such as the Centennial Park Concert for Life (TOP) or the annual City to Surf contest (BOTTOM), Sydney-siders are a close-knit bunch.

RANDWICK CITY COUNCIL

BY ORDER – GENERAL MANAGER

*S*IGNS OF THE TIMES: LIKE ANY other metropolitan center, Sydney has its share of little reminders to ensure that both traffic and people behave accordingly.

The mural text reads:

"THINK GLOBALY" ACT LOCALLY"
A COMMUNITY MURAL FOR PEACE
by PUBLIC ART SQUAD %
COMMISSIONED BY COUNCIL

PUBLIC ART SQUAD 1985

THE SENIOR MEMBERS OF SYDNEY'S population have mastered the art of relaxation—particularly as depicted on a Surry Hills wall mural.

B⸻ Farm, l⸻ an hour's drive from Sydney's central business district, is Australia's oldest surviving group of farm buildings. Occupying 1,600 hectares, the farm offers visitors the chance to ⸻ the rural life of the 1800s, from milking a cow to sampling wines in the vineyard. The farm has preserved its rustic ambience for more than 150 years.

Whether nestled underneath the trees of Bronte's St. Stephen's Cemetery or with a perpetual view of the water in Waverly Cemetery, the Sydney area's final resting places are picturesque and serene.

MOSMAN BAY, WITH ITS MOORED boats and rugged, leafy shores, has attracted people for more than 200 years. The quiet serenity of the cove is the perfect spot for a picnic and a stroll.

THE SCENIC ATTRACTIONS SUR-
rounding Sydney are plentiful.
Ku-ring-gai Chase National Park
(TOP) contains some of the most
important Aboriginal rock engrav-
ings and cave art in the area, and
the name itself is derived from a
former local tribe, the Guringai.
Beautiful Royal National Park
(OPPOSITE) and Mosman Bay (CEN-
TER) offer up pleasures of their own.

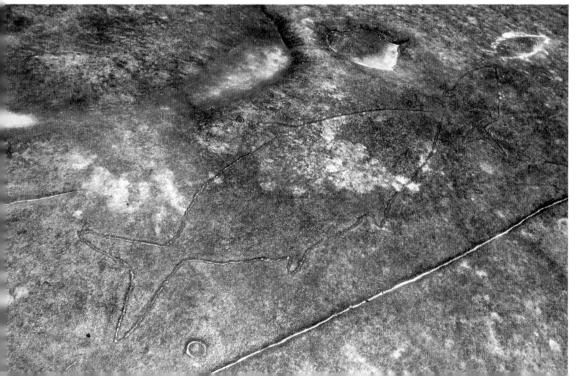

THE MYTHICAL QUALITY OF BLUE
Mountains National Park is ech-
oed as much in Wentworth Falls
(OPPOSITE BOTTOM) as in the Three
Sisters rock formation (LEFT).
According to an Aboriginal legend, three beautiful sisters were
turned into stone by a kind
witchdoctor in order to protect
them from a dangerous battle.
Although the witchdoctor perished
during the fighting, the sisters still
stand on their perch overlooking
the Jamison Valley.

FROM THE CLIFFS OF JAMISON
Valley to the rooftops of
Katoomba, wherever you are in
Blue Mountains National Park,
the view is breathtaking.

Held annually, Australian Fashion Week (ABOVE) brings Sydney into the international fashion circuit, alongside such posh locations as Milan, London, and New York. On a more individual level, it's the small shops around the city that help keep it beautiful.

On Bluey Day in Australia, police officers shave their heads to raise funds for children with cancer. Should the fad catch on, Sydney barber Pantaleo Scalone might experience a bit of a work slow-down. Not to worry: Maintaining Scalone's massive postcard collection is enough to keep him busy.

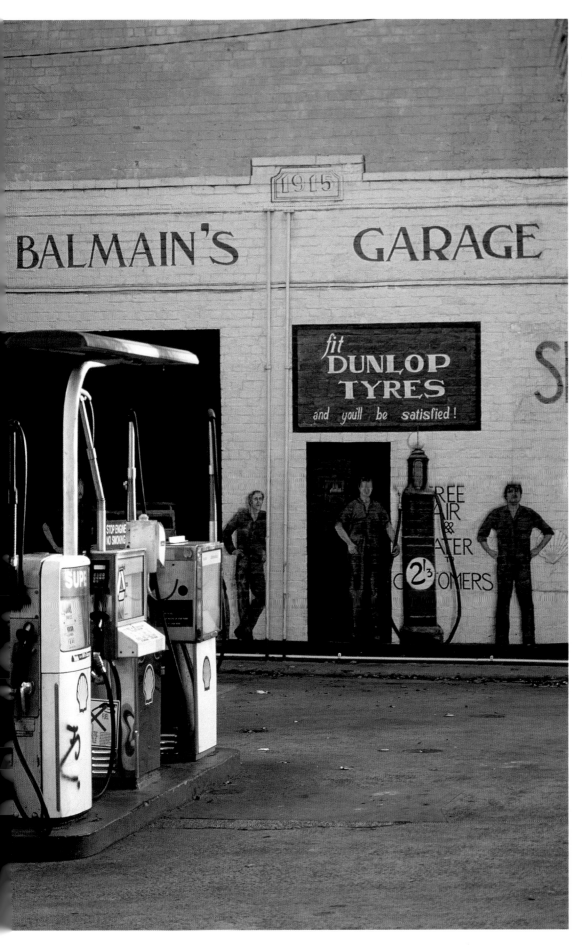

BALMAIN'S GARAGE

1915

fit DUNLOP TYRES
and you'll be satisfied!

Putting the finishing touches on vehicles that soar and sail, Sydneysiders take pride in their work.

'Food, just like everything else in Sydney life, revolves around the water. The mellow atmosphere that saturates its restaurants seduces patrons into taking full advantage of the excellent views, stimulating conversation, and plentiful wine.

WHARVES ARE AN INTEGRAL PART of Sydney's transportation system, serving as the base of operations for the ferries that carry people to and from different parts of the city. Recently, they have also become the subject of renovation and growth.

FRIEND IN HAND PUB OWNER
Peter Byrnes and his feathered
companion, Josephine, show that
friendship can take on many forms.
Beer and good food are in abun-
dance at Sydney's numerous eating
establishments, including the glitzy
Planet Hollywood (BOTTOM).

CARS AND SAILBOATS ARE NOT THE only modes of transportation in Sydney. Motorcyclists are increasing in numbers, from avid riders to weekend bikers. Yet no one can say they've seen Sydney without a visit to Harry's Cafe de Wheels, an institution since 1945.

ʃYDNEY'S BRIDGES HAVE A BEAUTY all their own. With their concrete supports and broad expanses of pavement, the Gladesville Bridge (OPPOSITE), Sydney Harbour Bridge (LEFT), and Cammeray Bridge (RIGHT) are feats of solid engineering. The steel cables of the Glebe Island Bridge (PAGES 194 AND 195) apparently found their inspiration in nature.

FROM BONDI BEACH TO GLEN Alpine, the suburban sprawl of Sydney is quite obvious from a bird's-eye view.

THE TERRACES AND VERANDAS OF
Sydney neighborhoods such as
Paddington and Kings Cross have
withstood the test of time, and
lend a romantic air to the rest of
the city.

THE WORKING-CLASS SUBURBS OF
Redfern (ABOVE) and Surry Hills
(OPPOSITE) had changed very little
until recent years. Today, Surry
Hills is home to a younger, bohe-

mian crowd, while Redfern is expe-
riencing its own chic resurgence.
Visitors to the Rocks district in
1960 (PAGE 203) were greeted by
the looming arch of the Sydney

Harbour Bridge. From a different
perspective, the Sydney Opera
House unfolds its wings in a
classic, modern-day view from
Kirribilli (PAGE 202).

With intricate, stone-carved detail and narrow alleys, The Rocks preserves Sydney's rich colonial history. Named after the cliffs that once dominated the area, The Rocks was the makeshift home of Australia's first settlers.

THE ROCKS SURVIVED FOR TWO centuries until plans arose to demolish the entire area to make way for sleeker, more modern buildings. After much protesting from Sydneysiders, the area was scrubbed and polished, instead, and now flourishes with its original old-world ambience.

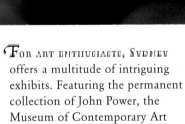

ᵀFOR ART ENTHUSIASTS, SYDNEY offers a multitude of intriguing exhibits. Featuring the permanent collection of John Power, the Museum of Contemporary Art (TOP LEFT) opened in 1991 at Circular Quay West. On weekends, the Rocks Market (OPPOSITE) is the place to go for unique arts and crafts. And every other year, Sydney holds the Biennale, showcasing avant-garde works at various locations throughout the city.

ALWAYS FLUID, DAY OR NIGHT and fueled by the energy of its people, Sydney is a city on the move.

Sydney
PROFILES IN EXCELLENCE

A LOOK AT THE CORPORATIONS, BUSINESSES, PROFESSIONAL GROUPS, AND COMMUNITY SERVICE ORGANISATIONS THAT HAVE MADE THIS BOOK POSSIBLE. THEIR STORIES—OFFERING AN INFORMAL CHRONICLE OF THE LOCAL BUSINESS COMMUNITY—ARE ARRANGED ACCORDING TO THE DATE THEY WERE ESTABLISHED IN SYDNEY.

AM Corporation Ltd. ❧ Amcor St. Regis Bates ❧ American Chamber of Commerce in Australia ❧ AON Risk Services Australia Limited ❧ AT&T Communications Services Australia Pty Limited ❧ Australian Business Limited ❧ Australian Gas Light Company ❧ Boeing Australia Limited ❧ CB Richard Ellis ❧ Citibank ❧ Clayton Utz ❧ Computer Associates International, Inc. ❧ Compuware Asia-Pacific Pty Ltd ❧ Corporate Relocations ❧ The Cox Group ❧ David Jones Limited ❧ FedEx ❧ Freehill Hollingdale & Page ❧ Gemtec Pty Ltd ❧ The Grace Hotel ❧ Grace Removals Group ❧ Hotel Nikko Darling Harbour/Sydney ❧ KvB Institute of Technology ❧ Liebert Corporation Australia ❧ Manpower Inc. ❧ Medtronic Australasia Pty. Ltd. ❧ Meinhardt (NSW) Pty Ltd ❧ Merrill Lynch (Australia) Pty Limited ❧ Michael Page International ❧ New South Wales Department of State and Regional Development ❧ Ord Minnett Group ❧ Paddy's Markets ❧ Preformed Line Products (Australia) Pty Ltd ❧ Radio 2UE ❧ St Vincent's Private Hospital ❧ State Chamber of Commerce (New South Wales) ❧ State Rail Authority of New South Wales ❧ Suzanne Grae Corporation Pty Ltd ❧ Sydney Adventist Hospital ❧ Sydney Convention & Visitors Bureau ❧ Sydney Marriott Hotel ❧ TAFE NSW ❧ Towery Publishing, Inc. ❧ United Airlines ❧ Walker Corporation Limited ❧ Westpac Banking Corporation ❧ WorldxChange Communications ❧ Young & Rubicam Inc.

1817-1970

1817	Westpac Banking Corporation
1825	State Chamber of Commerce (New South Wales)
1833	Clayton Utz
1837	Australian Gas Light Company
1838	David Jones Limited
1855	State Rail Authority of New South Wales
1869	Paddy's Markets
1871	Freehill Hollingdale & Page
1872	Ord Minnett Group
1883	TAFE NSW
1885	Australian Business Limited
1903	Sydney Adventist Hospital
1909	St Vincent's Private Hospital
1911	Grace Removals Group
1925	Amcor St. Regis Bates
1925	Radio 2UE
1938	Boeing Australia Limited
1961	American Chamber of Commerce in Australia
1966	CB Richard Ellis
1966	Manpower Inc.
1967	The Cox Group
1967	Preformed Line Products (Australia) Pty Ltd
1967	Walker Corporation Limited
1968	Suzanne Grae Corporation Pty Ltd
1969	Sydney Convention & Visitors Bureau
1969	Young & Rubicam Inc.

Westpac Banking Corporation

$\mathcal{E}$STABLISHED IN 1817 AS THE BANK OF NEW SOUTH WALES, Westpac Banking Corporation not only is Australia's first and oldest bank, but also is the first and oldest Australian company. As one of the four major banks operating across Australia today, Westpac takes pride in its many achievements over the course of a long and fruitful history. The bank strives to be first in delivering superior products and

customer service in the banking and financial industry.

On the Australian Stock Exchange, Westpac is ranked among the top 10 companies in market capitalisation. The company has more than 160,000 individual and institutional shareholders locally and around the world. Westpac's vision is to deliver better financial solutions to its customers.

International Presence

From its headquarters in Sydney's Martin Place, Westpac has developed a national and international presence. Westpac has a presence across Australia through various service points, including more than 1,000 branches, sub-branches, agencies, and service centres. The bank's network includes more than 1,300 automatic teller machines (ATMs) and 25,000 electronic funds transfer point-of-sale (EFTPOS) terminals.

Westpac concentrates its activities in Australia, New Zealand, and the Pacific Islands. It operates a regional banking approach, which delivers most of the customer-based decisions to regional banks.

In 1996, Westpac merged with Trust Bank New Zealand, further expanding its presence. In New Zealand, the newly named WestpacTrust operates through more than 300 branch offices and more than 400 ATMs. In addition, Westpac has branches, offices, or representative offices throughout Asia and the Pacific, as well as branches in New York and London. With a strong presence overseas, Westpac is a gateway for trade and commerce within and outside Australia.

Today, the banking industry is undergoing a transition, moving from branch-based transactions towards more electronic transactions, EFTPOS,

and telephone banking. For the cost of a local telephone call, telephone banking is available 24 hours a day, seven days a week from anywhere in Australia. Customers can also obtain balances, transfer money, or conduct other transactions over the Internet.

Bob Joss, Westpac CEO and Managing Director, describes the bank's staff of 30,000 as its greatest asset. In a major commitment to its employees, the bank has put in place a program that evaluates the training and professional development needs of each individual on a case-by-case

basis. Training is then provided not only to assist staff members in carrying out their jobs in a competent and professional manner, but also to train them for future roles within the bank's organisation.

A Wide Range of Services

Among Westpac's subsidiaries is Australian Guarantee Corporation (AGC). This wholly owned operation is Australia's largest finance company with more than $7 billion in assets. AGC's specialty is point-of-sale finance for consumer durables. In

FROM ITS HEADQUARTERS IN SYDNEY'S MARTIN PLACE, WESTPAC BANKING CORPORATION HAS DEVELOPED A NATIONAL AND INTERNATIONAL PRESENCE. IT IS ONE OF THE FOUR MAJOR BANKS OPERATING ACROSS AUSTRALIA TODAY (RIGHT).

BOB JOSS, WESTPAC CEO AND MANAGING DIRECTOR, DESCRIBES THE BANK'S STAFF OF 30,000 AS ITS GREATEST ASSET (BELOW).

S Y D N E

its wide array of services, AGC also offers personal and commercial finance, and asset-backed and working capital financial products.

Westpac Financial Services (WFS), one of the largest retail fund managers in Australia, is another wholly owned subsidiary. WFS exercises discretionary management for more than $17 billion in investment funds, as well as some $87 billion for which the company acts as custodian. Westpac Custodian Nominees executes more than 25,000 trade settlements each month and is the largest provider of such services in Australia.

WFS' broad range of investment offerings includes superannuation and insurance products and services. The general insurance division caters to the needs of more than 400,000 customers for personal, business, marine, primary products, and many other types of insurance. Two property portfolios, Westpac Property Trust and Industry Superannuation Property Trust, with total assets worth more than $1.5 billion, form part of the investment property division.

Specialising in Australian cash and fixed interests, Australian shares, and tactical asset allocation, the investment management division is wholly owned by WFS. The wholesale investment products range is extensive, with total client investments worth some $7.7 billion. The Australian shares investment protocol is value based.

The retail and business investment division provides financial advice and a comprehensive line of retail investment products, both excluding and including superannuation. Life and trauma insurance products have also been developed. The division has 450 staff members to assist

some 550,000 clients with selecting the most suitable products to best arrange their financial investments, which total some $4.9 billion under management.

A History of Leadership

The bank was founded in 1817 by New South Wales Governor Lachlan Macquarie. He saw that the recently settled colony could not prosper without a banking infrastructure to ensure a stable currency, as well as a financial system to facilitate commerce and trade. With support from the local population, but without official approval from London, Macquarie signed the bank's charter after a meeting of 13 selected citizens agreed to establish it. The directors included names prominent in Aus-

tralian history, including William Redfern and D'Arcy Wentworth.

With a pioneering spirit, the bank assisted in the economic development of Australia during both the difficult and the boom times. Through the establishment of a savings bank, Westpac was the first bank to offer housing loans to individuals and cooperative building societies, and it was the first private bank to operate a savings bank in Australia.

As Australia's first bank, Westpac strives to remain a leader in providing services to assist its many customers in meeting their comprehensive banking and financial needs. The bank's success is the result of its continuous efforts to understand its customers' needs and to develop products to meet them.

CLOCKWISE FROM TOP LEFT: WESTPAC HAS A PRESENCE ACROSS AUSTRALIA THROUGH VARIOUS SERVICE POINTS, INCLUDING MORE THAN 1,300 AUTOMATIC TELLER MACHINES.

AUSTRALIAN SWIMMING SENSATION AND WESTPAC-SPONSORED ATHLETE IAN THORPE (RIGHT) CHECKS OUT THE CURRENT EDITION OF O News, A WORLD-FIRST NATIONAL OLYMPIC GAMES SCHOOL NEWSPAPER, WITH SYDNEY PRIMARY SCHOOL STUDENT 11-YEAR-OLD MATTHEW HARRIGAN.

WESTPAC STAFF MEMBERS RAISE MONEY FOR WALK FOR THE CURE, A FUND-RAISING EVENT FOR JUVENILE DIABETES.

◄ C. MOORE HARDY, STARFISH STUDIO

ESTABLISHED IN 1825, THE STATE CHAMBER OF COMMERCE (New South Wales) is Australia's second oldest continuing organisation, and the oldest business association in the country. The State Chamber of Commerce is the peak employer body in New South Wales, with a charter designed to represent and support members in developing, promoting, and enhancing business life and commerce in the state.

The State Chamber's strength is the diversity of its membership base. The organisation refrains from being the voice of any one business sector, and has a purposeful determination to resolve the issues affecting its more than 100,000 businesses across the state from every industry and company size.

Resources are not limited to State Chamber staff. The networking opportunities among its members and more than 300 local chambers provide a vast database of skills, knowledge, and expertise.

History

In 1825, a group of Sydney merchant businessmen led by John Wollstonecraft established the Sydney Chamber of Commerce to give voice to the concerns of international traders and to lobby the government of the day. As the Sydney Chamber grew, it changed its name to reflect the needs of its growing membership and to promote its changing focus in covering state issues. The State Chamber has continued to grow, and unlike many of its sister state chambers and other business associations who have merged with similar organisations, the New South Wales State Chamber's strength and profile have enabled it to remain a strong and independent organisation.

Although the Chamber's office has been housed in different locations over the course of its long history, the headquarters has always remained within the mercantile district of Sydney. Today, the State Chamber has developed a modern, well-equipped work environment for its staff of more than 40 dedicated, high-calibre employees. As an incorporated company, the State Chamber is guided by a board of directors led by the organisation's chief executive officer.

Recognising Women

For the first time in its history, the State Chamber appointed a female chief executive in 1996, Katie Lahey. This milestone represented a change in the culture of the Chamber, and reflected the growing recognition that women play an increasingly important role in business and management.

To support this growing recognition, the State Chamber introduced the National Enterprising Women (NEW) program, an initiative to support women in establishing and succeeding in their own businesses and careers. Among the program's goals is to inform and educate the community, governments, media, and business sector on women's roles in contributing to the economic wealth of the country.

CLOCKWISE FROM TOP: LOBBYING ACTIVITIES, RESEARCH PAPERS, AND A STRONG MEMBERSHIP BASE ATTRACT ONGOING, HIGH-PROFILE MEDIA COVERAGE OF THE STATE CHAMBER OF COMMERCE (NEW SOUTH WALES).

THE STATE CHAMBER'S CHIEF EXECUTIVE, KATIE LAHEY, JOINED THE ORGANISATION IN 1996, AND HAS SET THE CHAMBER'S STRATEGIC DIRECTION FOR THE NEXT MILLENNIUM. AS A RESULT OF HER LEADERSHIP, MEMBERSHIP NUMBERS HAVE GROWN SIGNIFICANTLY AND NEW SERVICES HAVE BEEN DEVELOPED.

MANY OF THE STATE CHAMBER'S MEMBERS ARE LISTED ON THE AUSTRALIAN STOCK EXCHANGE.

JASON BUSCH, WILDLIGHT

Good Relations

A hallmark of the Chamber has always been its apolitical nature in maintaining an exceptionally good working relationship with all tiers of government, regardless of which party is in power. It remains a not-for-profit organisation and does not receive government funding.

The State Chamber is seen as a barometer for business. Governments seek its advice when developing new business and economic policies. The State Chamber is involved in policy submissions, and because of its diverse membership across a broad spectrum of industries, government bodies are assured of a diverse range of business opinions that could affect new policies and legislation.

Services

Since its inception, the State Chamber has evolved to meet the needs of its members in a competitive business environment by developing packages of products and services to facilitate business for its members. Members are surveyed regularly to gain their perspective on the prospects for business and the economy. These surveys provide the Chamber with a snapshot of its members' ever changing needs. This information and other quality research contribute to the formulation of policy statements and publications that secure media attention about relevant issues.

The State Chamber advises members on a variety of business issues. Free fact sheets are available on such subjects as franchising, marketing, business planning, and government related ventures. In addition, a panel of professional experts from member companies provides advice on specialised topics, from legal issues and accounting to taxation. The State Chamber's Industrial Relations Department provides in-depth services across the broad base of employment relations issues, from interpreting industrial awards and acts to advising members on employment contracts. Policy committees and forums, consisting of expert State Chamber members, formulate directions in lobbying for changes to legislation, as well as other aspects of business life.

The State Chamber organises a regular calendar of more than 100 events each year, where members can exchange ideas and canvass the opinions of the guest speakers who are

◀ PHILIP QUIRK, WILDLIGHT

◀ DAVID MOORE, WILDLIGHT

some of Australia's most prominent business leaders and decision makers.

International Presence

With its history as a world-class trading centre, Sydney is the prime launching pad for overseas expansion. The World Trade Centre Sydney is the State Chamber's international trade division and a gateway to successful international trade for local entrepreneurs. The World Trade Centre Sydney provides information, global contacts, assistance for exporting and importing, and links to more than 300 World Trade Centres in over 97 countries.

The State Chamber's profile enabled it to secure the rights to manage the Sydney 2000 Olympic Commerce Centre. A State Chamber initiative provides opportunities and advice to the business community in the lead-up to the Sydney 2000 Olympic Games. The centre will continue to be a valuable bank of knowledge, information, and expertise to assist and advise Australian businesses with regard to sourcing possible opportunities provided by future Olympics held overseas.

The Future

The key to continuing success for the State Chamber and its members is staying tuned-in to the developments and trends in the ever changing business environment. The Chamber is constantly developing new services that will enhance the potential for its members' success, both within the Australian business environment and in the worldwide marketplace of expanding opportunities.

THE STATE CHAMBER MAINTAINS THE SUPPORT OF THE MAJORITY OF CORPORATE MEMBERS, SUCH AS AMP, KPMG, AND AAPT, AND IS PROUD OF THE FACT THAT COMPANIES LIKE AMP HAVE BEEN ACTIVE MEMBERS FOR MORE THAN 80 YEARS (TOP).

THE STATE CHAMBER'S INTERNATIONAL TRADE DEPARTMENT, THE WORLD TRADE CENTRE SYDNEY, ASSISTS ITS MEMBERS IN TAKING ADVANTAGE OF SYDNEY'S STATUS AS AN INTERNATIONAL GATEWAY TO AUSTRALIA AND THE WORLD. THE STATE CHAMBER CONTINUES TO CAMPAIGN FOR SYDNEY TO RETAIN ITS WORKING HARBOUR (BOTTOM).

PHOTOGRAPHY PROVIDED BY STATE CHAMBER MEMBER WILDLIGHT PHOTO AGENCY PTY LTD

Clayton Utz

CLAYTON UTZ, A FULL-SERVICE COMMERCIAL LAW FIRM, PROVIDES legal advice and assistance for organisations in Australia and throughout the world. With offices in the major commercial centres—Melbourne, Brisbane, Perth, Canberra, and Darwin—the firm's national headquarters is located in Sydney, Australia's major commercial centre. Today, Clayton Utz has a team of more than 185 partners and 600 other legal practitioners,

supported by more than 700 additional personnel. Its offices are linked electronically by the latest high-technology systems.

Clayton Utz proudly traces its heritage back to 1833, when George Robert Nichols—the first Australian-born solicitor—was admitted to the New South Wales Bar. In 1920, the firms of John H. Clayton & Son and Mackenzie and Mackenzie, conducted by Harold Stewart Utz, amalgamated as Clayton & Utz. The practice has seen many prominent Sydney citizens among its number, including politicians and war heroes. The firm changed its name to Clayton Utz in 1983, and the establishment of an office in Melbourne the same year began a period of unprecedented expansion that continues to this day.

A Dynamic Law Firm

"Dynamic" is the word that Clayton Utz uses to describe its core value and the spirit that guides its approach to client service. "At Clayton Utz, we believe in giving our clients a unique and vital advantage. We have a passion for bringing fresh thinking to the legal and commercial challenges of today's ever changing business environment, and for quickly grasping the implications of new laws," says the firm's positioning statement. "Ours is a pragmatic approach providing energy, action, and effective solutions. We call it dynamic law."

The practice is centred on four main areas: corporate, litigation and dispute resolution, banking and finance, and property and construction. The breadth of law covered in its 22 national industry/practice groups, ranges from competition law and product liability to telecommunications, health, and workplace relations law. With the experience garnered from its years of work in all areas of commercial activity, Clayton Utz is proud of the breadth and depth of experience that it can bring to bear on behalf of clients.

In addition to Australian businesses—including mining, banking, insurance, automotive, pharmaceutical, telecommunications, and energy production companies—the firm serves foreign-owned corporations with international operations, as well as domestic businesses with purely local interests. The firm's client list includes such industry leaders as AAPT, ACI Packaging, Boral, BTR plc, Cable & Wireless, Coca-Cola Amatil, CSR, Email, Seven Network TNT, Toyota, and all of the major banks. Additionally, the firm counsels a number of public sector clients, including government departments, statutory authorities, and government business enterprises.

Team of Professionals

The firm's personnel are selected for their intelligence, teamwork, understanding of the law, capacity

for hard work, and ability to develop effective solutions quickly. To develop the depth of support that distinguishes the firm, Clayton Utz has in place a program of continuous internal and external training and education programs for all its personnel.

Rotation between the firm's different practice groups enriches the understanding and competence of its personnel, enabling them to appreciate the complexities of clients' various business environments. In addition, the Clayton Utz program of secondment to clients, other Clayton Utz offices, and overseas law firms helps the firm's team of professionals develop realistic and practical legal solutions. Additionally, personnel in all offices can instantaneously communicate with one another, share information, and seek advice through high-speed modem access.

International

Clayton Utz has an international presence through two prestigious networks of independent law firms. Clayton Utz is a founding member of the Pacific Rim Advisory Council, which connects major law firms from around the world and gives Clayton Utz a presence in more than 20 commercial centres throughout the

Pacific Rim. In addition, the firm is a member of Lex Mundi, a global association of more than 150 independent law firms. Many Australian companies having operations overseas have found that their legal interests are best served when Clayton Utz lawyers coordinate legal activities from the firm's Australian base, with local legal practitioners—many of whom are pre-eminent in their field—performing the work.

By immersing itself in the business of its clients, Clayton Utz develops a close understanding of their needs. With a dynamic approach to its work, the firm develops practical solutions that bring success to clients, as well as to the firm itself. Dynamism and a close relationship with clients are the qualities that have been identified by Clayton Utz as necessary for assisting clients in achieving success in a legally complex business environment.

Australian Gas Light Company

The Australian Gas Light Company (AGL), a multifaceted, listed public energy company, is Australia's primary supplier of both gas and electricity. More than 1.5 million customers depend on AGL for their energy needs, from the humblest households to the largest businesses. In addition, the company is expanding on the world market through the acquisition of interests in both energy concerns and related

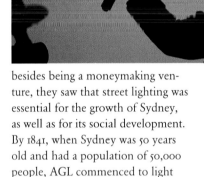

CLOCKWISE FROM TOP: AUSTRALIAN GAS LIGHT COMPANY (AGL) IS THE COUNTRY'S LEADING ENERGY COMPANY TRADING IN NATURAL GAS, ELECTRICITY, AND LIQUEFIED PETROLEUM GAS (LPG).

ELGAS LTD, 50 PER CENT OWNED BY AGL, IS CURRENTLY CONSTRUCTING A 65,000-TONNE UNDERGROUND LPG STORAGE CAVERN NEAR SYDNEY'S PORT BOTANY. A TECHNOLOGICAL FIRST FOR AUSTRALIA TO PROVIDE A SECURE ENERGY SUPPLY TO ELGAS' GROWING CUSTOMER BASE.

AGL'S RAPID EXPANSION SEES THE COMPANY INVOLVED IN MAJOR PROJECTS BUILDING INFRASTRUCTURE AND DISTRIBUTING, MARKETING, AND RETAILING ENERGY THROUGHOUT AUSTRALIA AND OVERSEAS.

high-tech manufacturing industries overseas, as well as through partnerships with governments and energy industry leaders.

The company's market capitalisation stands at about $3.8 billion, currently the 29th largest on the Australian Stock Exchange. The oldest company in Australia to still trade under its original name, AGL has 326 million issued ordinary shares, and is owned by more than 44,000 proprietors. Ninety-eight per cent of its staff are shareholders.

History

A group of Sydney entrepreneurs formed AGL in 1837 under a charter granted by King William IV, making it one of the oldest gas companies in the world. The founders of AGL had both a commercial and a civic impetus in establishing the company—

besides being a moneymaking venture, they saw that street lighting was essential for the growth of Sydney, as well as for its social development. By 1841, when Sydney was 50 years old and had a population of 50,000 people, AGL commenced to light the streets of the city.

This strong sense of civic duty has remained at the core of the company throughout its long history. In the first 100 years of Sydney's history, gas was the predominantly used fuel, driving industry and bringing new enterprises to the city. Gas

made it possible for new business ventures to develop manufacturing processes for metals, brick, glass, and other vital products. In 1858, the state government legislated that AGL could operate anywhere in the state, acknowledging the success of the company in meeting the needs of people and satisfying the high standards of good business conduct.

In the 1870s, AGL expanded its services to include supplying gas for cooking, and later for hot-water services and home heating. In expanding its services, AGL developed

a sophisticated reticulation system for distributing gas throughout the Sydney metropolitan area.

Over its long history, AGL has overcome difficulties, including competition from electricity, and has enjoyed many successes. One triumph for the company was the massive conversion of all its customers to natural gas in 1978.

AGL Today

AGL has grown to become a major force in the Australian energy industry. The company owns natural gas distribution networks in New South Wales and the Australian Capital Territory, and owns or operates 8,500 kilometres of transmission pipelines across the country. In New Zealand, AGL manages the distribution and retailing activities of the Natural Gas Corporation, which has 50,000 customers.

In sales and marketing, AGL has 800,000 natural gas customers and a combined total of 1 million gas and electricity customers. AGL retails and wholesales gas, liquid petroleum gas (LPG), and related services. It owns 50 per cent of Elgas Ltd, which has 250,000 customers, and all of HC Extractions, which has achieved annual LPG production of more than 36,500 tonnes. AGL owns an electricity distribution network covering nearly 8,000 square kilometres of the Greater Melbourne area, and retails electricity to around 25,000 customers. Through its program of global expansion, AGL has acquired one-third of Natural Gas Corporation in New Zealand, including 2,600 kilometres of transmission pipelines.

Through a joint venture in Chile called Gas Valpo, AGL has expanded overseas in a move that carries the potential for significant growth. AGL anticipates this enterprise will demonstrate the capacities of the company as a leader in the energy industry beyond its home ground. In addition, the venture will also present an opportunity to demonstrate the cutting-edge nylon natural gas pipe technology which the company has developed through Industrial Pipeline Systems (IPS), a wholly owned subsidiary that manufactures specialty pipes.

Green Citizen

As a business that provides a vital service to the community, AGL also prides itself on being a socially responsible company.

The AGL Foundation, established in 1987 during the company's 150th anniversary, supports charities beneficial to the community. In addition, AGL sponsors the Clean Up Australia and Greening Australia campaigns, is a member of the Greenhouse Challenge, and actively supports the Sustainable Energy Development Authority. The Sydney and Dubbo zoos are among other recipients of the company's financial support.

AGL's primary short-term goal is to continue expansion across Australia by winning more customers through packages designed to meet the energy needs of each individual customer. Evolving into a world-class energy company, AGL is also in an excellent position to increase its investments and operations overseas. Building on its proud reputation as a reliable and cost-effective provider of energy for more than a century, Australian Gas Light Company looks forward to further growth in the new millennium.

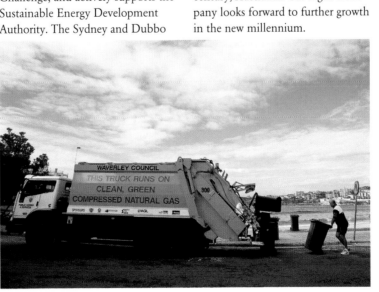

David Jones Limited

David Jones Limited proudly wears the mantle of Australia's premier department store, recognised especially for its exclusive range of fashion and home wares. Driven by high standards, the company has traditionally set the benchmark for quality retailing in Australia. The flagship store on Elizabeth Street in Sydney epitomises a luxurious shopping experience.

Established in 1838, just 50 years after the founding of the colony of New South Wales, David Jones is Australia's oldest department store, as well as the oldest store in the world still trading under its original name. Today, David Jones has grown into a national retail chain of some 29 stores.

The values that have bolstered the company throughout its history are today encapsulated in its mission statement: "David Jones is driven by a desire to provide customers with world-class service, quality, style, and choice, and in turn to provide increased returns to shareholders."

History of an Australian Institution

The store was named after its founder, David Jones, who was born in Wales and trained to work in the drapery trade in London. In Sydney, on the corner of George and Barrack streets, Jones opened a shop to sell buckskins, ginghams, waistcoat fabrics, silks, cotton ticks, diaper rugs, and other merchandise imported from England.

The business prospered, but when Jones' partners took over the management following his retirement from active business, the store failed. Although Jones lost everything, he came out of retirement at the age of 67, borrowed heavily, and—with the help of his son, Edward—managed to re-create the store's success. Edward introduced the European concept of the department store, which included the sale of furniture and furnishings, and saw the business flourish.

David Jones has met and surmounted other challenges over its long history. By implementing new initiatives and strategies, and by remaining true to the values that built David Jones, it has retained its premier position in Australian retailing.

The company is credited with achieving a number of firsts in Australian retailing. For more than a century, David Jones' mail-order department served Australians in every corner of the continent. The now famous fashion parades associated with David Jones were a first for Australia, when Paris fashions were showcased for Sydneysiders. The first time that Dior showed a collection outside Paris, it was at David Jones' Elizabeth Street store in 1949. Today, David Jones buyers search the world, as well as Australia to select a broad range of the highest-quality merchandise.

Improvements in Store

In the late 1990s, David Jones conducted a major review of all its store in order to enhance service and financial performance. Under a program

ESTABLISHED IN 1838, JUST 50 YEARS AFTER THE FOUNDING OF THE COLONY OF NEW SOUTH WALES, DAVID JONES IS AUSTRALIA'S OLDEST DEPARTMENT STORE, AS WELL AS THE OLDEST STORE IN THE WORLD STILL TRADING UNDER ITS ORIGINAL NAME. THE FLAGSHIP STORE ON ELIZABETH STREET IN SYDNEY EPITOMISES A LUXURIOUS SHOPPING EXPERIENCE.

A WORLD-CLASS STANDARD OF CUS-
TOMER SERVICE AND A RANGE OF
QUALITY GOODS HAVE ALWAYS
BEEN INTEGRAL TO THE SUCCESS
OF DAVID JONES.

THE ELIZABETH STREET STORE'S PARK
TERRACE RESTAURANT OFFERS FINE
DINING.

of refurbishment, major renovations were completed in many stores throughout the chain.

A number of new stores have been opened in locations around Australia, including the Gold Coast. The company plans to open more stores, marking a confident geographical expansion. This is an essential part of the company's strategy to increase market share and fuel profitability through growth.

David Jones strives to foster an environment in which employees are empowered to contribute the best of their best abilities in a total team effort. In the drive to achieve world-class standards, David Jones fosters the skills of all its 8,000 staff members through specially designed training programs. All salespeople complete a special training program focusing on the needs of customers. The aim of the internationally recognised program is to achieve consistency in service quality throughout the chain.

Central to the success of David Jones is the expertise of the buying team. Recognising that buying is a skill that is cultivated over time, David Jones has in place programs to nurture the talents of these staff members and to attract trainees.

Community Spirit

David Jones makes available promotional space for many large organisations that it supports, including the Breast Cancer Foundation, and has held special fundraising exhibitions for charities. In addition, the Donation Committee allocates sponsorship funding to many local fundraising activities supported by David Jones. As part of its commitment to fostering young Australian talent, the company stages a major window exhibition of student art each year.

Special events that have evolved into traditions over the years have made the Elizabeth Street store the focus of attention, giving it a recognised edge over its competitors. Each year Sydneysiders are treated to a burst of colour and fragrance in the David Jones Spring Flower Show, a celebration of flowers that is unmatched in Australia and is considered by many to be a must-see event. In addition, David Jones' annual Christmas window displays come alive through innovative designs and have captured the imaginations of Sydneysiders, making a visit to the store at Christmas an annual family event.

A world-class standard of customer service and a range of quality goods have always been integral to the success of David Jones. As an Australian shopping institution, David Jones has developed a reputation for quality, style, and good taste that resonates in a longstanding promotional slogan: "There's no other store like David Jones."

State Rail Authority of New South Wales

STATE RAIL AUTHORITY OF NEW SOUTH WALES (SRA) WAS established in 1855 following the demise of the privately owned Sydney Railway Company. Today, functioning through four operating divisions, the SRA offers passenger rail services throughout the state. Its board of directors is responsible for the organisation's performance and strategic direction, determining policies and ensuring that activities are carried

out properly and efficiently. SRA recognises that transportation is a key issue for the successful economic development of New South Wales, and that rail has a crucial role to play, not just in the efficient movement of people to their places of work and recreation, but in enhancing the functioning of the community and minimising the effects of transport on the environment.

CityRail

Carrying nearly 1 million passengers on more than 2,300 daily services in Sydney and the surrounding regions, the SRA's CityRail commuter network is one of the world's largest. CityRail trains offer extensive coverage of the region, travelling north to the Central Coast and Hunter Valley, west to the Blue Mountains, and south to the Southern Highlands and South Coast areas. Recent milestones include the provision of rail transport to Homebush Bay, the site of the Sydney 2000 Olympics and the new home of the historic Royal Easter Show, Australia's largest

annual event. On the busiest day of the first Royal Easter Show at Homebush Bay, CityRail carried 36,108 people per hour.

CityRail manages more than 300 stations, operates more than 2,060 kilometres of track, and utilises a fleet of more than 1,300 carriages. Sydney and the surrounding regions are served by double-deck electric trains, while the remainder of the CityRail network is served mainly by Endeavour diesel railcars. Preparations for rail transport during the upcoming Olympic Games was begun early, including the establishment of a special committee to monitor progress of planning and work, and to address emerging issues.

Beyond special events, CityRail has committed itself to providing day-to-day services that are accessible to everyone. Under the Easy Access program, for example, three dozen CityRail stations have already been improved for use by people with disabilities, and plans have been prepared that will guide the long-term development of new and existing facilities. Lifts and low-gradient

ramps are currently being installed at the stations, and ramps for access to trains have already been provided. Induction loops for the hearing impaired are also being installed with the renovation of ticket offices.

In a program designed to improve passenger safety, the SRA identified risks through audits, which helped in developing relevant policies and strategies. Safety at stations was improved with a number of initiatives,

CLOCKWISE FROM TOP:
CITYRAIL'S BLACKTOWN STATION IN SYDNEY'S WESTERN SUBURBS SERVES AS A MAJOR RAIL LINE AND BUS INTERCHANGE.

CITYRAIL'S SYDNEY SUBURBAN NETWORK IS SERVICED BY A FLEET OF OVER 1,000 DOUBLE-DECK CARRIAGES.

CIRCULAR QUAY STATION IS LOCATED RIGHT ON SYDNEY'S DOORSTEP. THIS STATION PLAYS A MAJOR ROLE DURING SPECIAL EVENTS.

GRAHAM MONRO

including the installation of video surveillance cameras and high-intensity lighting, the stationing of security guards on every train after 7 p.m., and the extension of the existing Nightsafe program. In addition, a commitment to maintaining high-quality environmental standards has led the SRA to develop and implement a certifiable environmental management system.

Countrylink

The SRA's long-distance passenger service is provided by Countrylink. The fleet, consisting primarily of high-speed XPT and Xplorer trains, travels more than 5.4 million kilometres each year. The service has some 350 destinations within and outside the state, including the Australian Capital Territory (ACT), Queensland, and Victoria. Additionally, a bus network supports the rail offerings in some locations. The popular Countrylink service has won a number of honours, including an ACT Tourism Award

for Major Transport Operators and recognition by the Australian Federation of Travel Agents as Best Transport Operator. Countrylink has also been a finalist in the New South Wales Tourism Awards. SRA's CityRail and Countrylink groups are supported by its Passenger Fleet Maintenance and Operations divisions.

History

Formed in 1849 and led by prominent pastoralist and politician Charles Cowper, the SRA's privately owned predecessor quickly faced financial difficulties. It was taken over by the New South Wales colonial government on September 3, 1855, and became the first publicly owned railway in the British Empire. Building on a consensus that rail development could overcome the region's poor road and communications infrastructure, the SRA opened the colony's first train service—a 22-kilometre line between Sydney and Parramatta—on September 26, 1855.

▲ GRAHAM MONRO

Over the years, the railways proved to be a significant catalyst for expansion and economic development in the colony, which later became the premier state in Australia. Expansion of the SRA system required many extraordinary feats of engineering that inspire awe even today. On the western outskirts of Sydney, for example, the railway climbed 1,118 metres to the entrance of the Clarence Tunnel, and then continued down a zigzag into the Lithgow Valley, traversing wondrous landscapes. Constructed in 1863, the SRA's original wrought-iron box-girder bridge at Menangle remains in use as the oldest railway span in Australia.

With the involvement of management, the board, and staff at all levels, the SRA continues to evolve strategies to advance its development. This approach has seen the SRA maintain its central role in the development of New South Wales and win the recognition of people as a responsible, customer-oriented passenger rail organisation.

▲ GRAHAM MONRO

CLOCKWISE FROM TOP:
A DRIVER VIEWS THE LINES AHEAD.

CITYRAIL'S DOUBLE-DECK INTERCITY TRAINS SERVICE REGIONAL CENTRES ON THE CITYRAIL NETWORK, INCLUDING GOSFORD ON THE NEWCASTLE & CENTRAL COAST LINE.

CITYRAIL MOVES NEARLY 1 MILLION CUSTOMERS PER DAY OVER SOME 2,600 KILOMETRES OF TRACK.

Paddy's Markets

Paddy's Markets was established in 1869 and has mirrored the history of the commercial and economic development of Sydney. Operating alongside Sydney's produce market in the early years of the colony, Paddy's Markets became a collection of vendors' stands dealing in a variety of wares, including second-hand goods, clothing, trinkets, and toys. ✦ Paddy's Markets has today become a popular

destination for shoppers of all kinds in Australia's oldest city. Sydneysiders and tourists alike frequent Paddy's Markets, taking in the local colour and the excitement of the markets, as vendors shout to advertise their arrays of goods, competing with one another to make sales. Paddy's Markets is located in Sydney's Central Business District, in the Haymarket precinct, and at Flemington, near the site of the Sydney 2000 Olympic Games.

A Long Tradition
History has not recorded the origins of Paddy's Markets' name, but historians suggest that the name is derived from the common parlance reference for the Chinese, who sup-

plied most of the produce of the market in its early days, or for the Irish, who formed the majority of its customers then. Others suggest the name was borrowed from England's well-known Paddy's Markets in the Irish area of Liverpool, since many of Sydney's early emigrants came from Liverpool, as well as from Ireland. By 1880, the markets had become an attraction. Offering a bazaar atmosphere and a unique shopping experience in the colony, it was a must-see for visitors from the bush and overseas.

The markets have been housed in several locations within the city's limits over its long history, but the stand holders have remained loyal, and they are the markets' driving force.

When the markets were threatened with closure in the early 1980s to make way for modern redevelopment, the stand holders rallied successfully to save this well-established landmark.

Convenience and Bargains
Open on Fridays, Saturdays, and Sundays, Paddy's at Haymarket is easily accessible by public transport through the Monorail, the Sydney Explorer bus, and Sydney Light Rail. The ground floor of the Market City shopping centre is home to Paddy's Haymarket; in the upstairs area, shoppers can enjoy coffee before again joining the throng of bargain hunters. Chinatown is within walking distance, as is the Darling Harbour complex.

At Paddy's Market bartering with stand holders is half the fun of bargain hunting (left).

Flemington Produce, one of the many stand holders at Paddy's Markets, offers fruits and vegetables straight from the heart of Sydney's wholesale produce markets (right).

▲▼ SYDNEY MARKETS LIMITED

Paddy's at Flemington has free parking facilities for thousands of cars. Although a railway station is within walking distance, 80 per cent of shoppers drive to the markets to take advantage of great prices on bulk fruit and vegetables. Paddy's at Flemington, open for business on Fridays and Sundays, is housed in Market Building D of the Sydney Markets, the city's fruit and vegetable wholesale markets. The two Paddy's Markets combined are the biggest retail markets in Sydney, and are known for their competitive prices.

While many of the stands have been handed down through generations of stand holders, keeping abreast of changing market trends for innovative products is also a tradition at Paddy's. More than 20,000 visitors each week take advantage of the unique Paddy's shopping experience to search out

bargains at the 1,000 stands at each location.

With a cornucopia of goods, home wares, and produce, Paddy's is a shopper's paradise. Stand holders have on display a variety of fresh fruits and vegetables, seafood, and meats. Bargain hunters will find the latest fashions in clothing and footwear. The markets are the ideal place for buying gifts, such as jewellery, leather goods, toys, plants, fresh flowers, novelties, and trinkets. Household goods, cosmetics, and even pets are on sale. Overseas visitors are well provided for, with a variety of souvenirs in all shapes and sizes, including boomerangs, sheepskin rugs, and toy kangaroos and koalas.

A trip to Paddy's at the weekend has become part of Sydney's shopping culture. Market research shows that a quarter of the city's population visits Paddy's every six months,

while tourists, both international and national, form 20 per cent of Paddy's customer base at Haymarket. Sydneysiders, irrespective of the frequency of their own visits to Paddy's, often take their tourist guests there.

Secure Future

The future of Paddy's Markets is secure, following its corporatisation in 1997, which made stand holders shareholders in Sydney Markets Limited. Secure leases mean stability for stand holders, and profits from the company are reinvested in the improvement of the sites and operations of the markets.

Paddy's continues to attract visitors and shoppers, who haggle for a bargain as in no other retail outlet in the city. The markets' slogan, "You haven't been to market 'til you've been to Paddy's" is an apt one, reflecting the unique nature of this colourful traditional Sydney marketplace.

CLOCKWISE FROM TOP: TAKEAWAY FOOD, SUCH AS THAT OFFERED BY THE DONER KEBAB VAN, IS ALWAYS POPULAR WITH VISITORS.

STUFFED TOY KOALAS AND FLAGS ARE AMONG THE MANY QUALITY AUSTRALIAN SOUVENIRS FOUND AT PADDY'S MARKETS.

TRADITIONAL AUSTRALIAN AKUBRA HATS ARE SOLD BY MANY STAND HOLDERS.

'FREEHILL HOLLINGDALE & PAGE HAS GROWN FROM A FAMILY legal practice founded in Sydney in 1871 to become one of the largest commercially oriented law firms in Australia and South-East Asia. Since its earliest days, the firm has maintained its prominence on the Sydney legal landscape. ❧ In Australia, Freehill Hollingdale & Page has offices in Sydney, Melbourne, Perth, Brisbane, and

Canberra. The firm's international network is powered by a total of 210 partners, 450 other attorneys, and 700 additional staff members. Since the early 1980s, when it was the first Australian law firm to invest in the development of an Asian regional practice, Freehill Hollingdale & Page has opened international offices in Hanoi and Ho Chi Minh City, and has developed a close professional affiliation with the firm of Soemadipradja & Taher in Jakarta. In the late 1990s, Freehills was ranked as the top legal adviser on mergers and acquisitions in Australia, having advised clients on some 60 transactions worth more than $20.3 billion, which represents nearly 50 per cent of the country's total market sector.

"OUR LAWYERS IN SYDNEY ACT FOR BOTH THE PUBLIC AND THE PRIVATE SECTOR, WITH CLIENTS RANGING FROM STATE AND FEDERAL REGULATORY BODIES TO LARGE TRANSNATIONAL AND MULTINATIONAL ORGANISATIONS," SAYS FREEHILL HOLLINGDALE & PAGE'S MANAGING PARTNER BRUCE CUTLER (PICTURED ABOVE).

Sydney Office

The Sydney office is the firm's largest, and its location in the international business capital of Australia gives Freehill Hollingdale & Page an ideal vantage point for handling the local, national, and international needs of clients. The nine main practice groups in the Sydney office cater to the diversified legal needs of clients. Practice areas include banking and finance, intellectual property, information technology and telecommunications, employment and industrial relations, commercial property services, corporate and commercial services, litigation, managed funds, and project and resource services, among other specialities.

In addition, Freehills Patent Attorneys, a separate but aligned service entity, provides specialist trademark and patent advice. Together with Freehill Hollingdale & Page, Freehills Patent Attorneys has developed an enviable reputation in the area of contested litigation. The firm has been involved in a number of high-profile product liability and trademark disputes.

Freehill Hollingdale & Page bring together lawyers with relevant expertise into focus groups that can develop the best strategies for the firm's clients. "Our lawyers in Sydney act for both the public and the private sector, with clients ranging from state and federal regulatory bodies t large transnational and multinational organisations," says Managing Partner

Bruce Cutler. Representing some of Australia's best-known organisations and companies, Freehill Hollingdale & Page has participated in landmark cases in areas such as corporate mergers and acquisitions, public floats, industrial relations, intellectual property, and litigation, to name but a few.

The Sydney office is staffed by more than 70 partners, some 200 solicitors and paralegals, and nearly 300 administrative staff members. The calibre of projects that Freehill Hollingdale & Page undertakes on behalf of its clients has made it possible for the firm to attract the highest-quality practitioners available in the legal profession.

History

The firm essentially remained a family firm from 1871 through to the 1930s, when it expanded into the commercial and corporate activities that are now its strength. The traditional values of respect and integrity in all dealings have underpinned the reputation and success of Freehill Hollingdale & Page.

Technology

The application of leading edge technology is a key feature of the added value that clients receive from Freehill Hollingdale & Page. Electronic databases provide fast and comprehensive tools that enable lawyers to conduct thorough legal research.

All staff members have direct access to the Internet not only for research purposes, but also for improved communications with clients. Developments such as video-conferencing, multimedia training, and use of electronic mobile time-management devices continue to improve communication with and accessibility to clients.

Pro Bono

Freehill Hollingdale & Page has always had a commitment to helping the disadvantaged in the community. In 1992, this commitment was formalised with the formation of the Pro Bono Committee and the establishment of formal guidelines for accepting pro bono work. Staff across all sections of the firm contribute to pro bono work, delivering services both in-house and at a number of external venues, such as the

IN AUSTRALIA, FREEHILL HOLLINGDALE & PAGE HAS OFFICES IN SYDNEY, MELBOURNE, PERTH, BRISBANE, AND CANBERRA. THE FIRM'S INTERNATIONAL NETWORK IS POWERED BY A TOTAL OF 210 PARTNERS, 450 OTHER ATTORNEYS, AND 700 ADDITIONAL STAFF MEMBERS.

Shopfront Youth Legal Centre in the Sydney suburb of Darlinghurst, which provides legal services to clients who are financially or otherwise disadvantaged.

The vision of the firm's founders remains the core of Freehill Hollingdale & Page: providing clients with the best commercial and strategic legal work that is relevant to their needs, and that is delivered by innovative teams in a way that exceeds market expectations in attention, cost effectiveness, clarity, simplicity, and timeliness. Freehill Hollingdale & Page's expertise, industry awareness, leadership, and innovative approaches will continue to be key to the firm's success in finding effective legal solutions for local and overseas clients well into the new millennium.

Ord Minnett Group

ORD MINNETT HAS A HISTORY THAT REACHES BACK MORE THAN a century. Formed by the amalgamation of three longstanding and respected stockbroking firms—T.J. Thompson & Sons, founded in 1872; A.W. Harvey, Lowe & Co, founded in 1932; and Charles A. Ord and Minnett, founded in 1949—the firm's reputation for being one of the most highly regarded broking and investment advisory houses in Australia is based on a bedrock of providing high-quality advice through its teams of advisers. Through its extensive retail network, Ord

ORD MINNETT IS LOCATED IN THE GROSVENOR BUILDING IN THE HISTORIC ROCKS AREA OF SYDNEY (TOP).

PICTURED BELOW ARE SOME KEY ORD MINNETT EXECUTIVES, INCLUDING (CLOCKWISE FROM TOP LEFT) CHRISTOPHER GORMAN, MANAGING DIRECTOR; PETER MASON, CHAIRMAN; PETER HERINGTON, FINANCE DIRECTOR; AND CHARLES MOORE, HEAD OF PRIVATE CLIENT INVESTMENT SERVICES.

Minnett encourages a close rapport between its advisers—who are respected throughout the industry for their knowledge, expertise, and experience—and its clients.

Today, Ord Minnett staff owns half of the company, and Jardine Fleming, an international financial services company, owns the remaining half. Jardine Fleming, in turn, is wholly owned by Robert Fleming, one of London's oldest and most prestigious investment banks.

Ord Minnett has global representation through the wider Fleming group and has a presence in New Zealand, San Francisco, Singapore, Hong Kong, New York, and London. These alliances benefit Ord Minnett clients in Australia and New Zealand, as well as internationally, by providing access to one of the world's most comprehensive networks of financial knowledge and services. The Australian headquarters of the company is located in the historic Rocks area of Sydney, Australia's financial capital and Olympic city.

Expertise
The organisation offers clients an array of services through its many business divisions. Independent surveys of the financial media over the last 25 years have consistently ranked Ord Minnett as one of the top three Australian institutional brokers. The company is proud to say that judging by market opinion and surveys, its Institutional Broking division provides one of the best research facilities in Australia to the top institutional fund managers.

With extensive experience in facilitating some of Australia's largest floats, mergers, and acquisitions, the group is highly respected. The Corporate Finance division was a joint domestic lead manager of Australia's largest initial public offering in the Telstra float in November 1997.

As one of the first and oldest retail brokers to be established in Australia, the company has developed one of the nation's most respected private client advisory networks. Major offices outside Sydney are located in Brisbane, Melbourne, Adelaide, Perth, Busselton, Bunbury, Orange, Mackay, Buderim, Gold Coast, Cairns, and Canberra. Ord Minnett is also well established in New Zealand with offices in Auckland, Wellington, and Christchurch.

Through its 16 retail offices around Australasia, the company is able to work closely with its clients to build an understanding and trust that cannot be achieved through electronic communications. Building a strong, personal relationship with its clients is a trademark quality of Ord Minnett.

The Futures division is one of the largest brokers operating in Australia's premier futures market through the Sydney Futures Exchange. Through Ord Minnett, clients have 24-hour access to the world's futures markets.

The funds management arm, Ord Minnett Investments is a world leader in structuring and marketing strategic investments, and has now raised more than $550 million from a series of innovative managed funds. Each fund is structured to provide diversification from traditional investments in shares, property, and bonds, while providing the security of a rising capital guarantee from the Westpac Banking Corporation.

Ord Minnett's Cash Management Fund, where clients place funds on deposit, now has more than $400 million under management. Leveraged Equities, another wholly owned subsidiary, supplies financing for clients to purchase share portfolios that, in turn, serve as security for these loans. The division has lent more than $700 million to Australian investors, secured by more than $1.5 billion in shares and managed funds. Leveraged Equities distributes its products through 85 stockbroking houses and numerous financial planning intermediaries around Australia. It is the second-largest margin-lending company in Australia.

Ord Minnett Investment Planning caters to individuals looking for a broader range of investment planning services. Clients receive specialist advice on superannuation, retirement planning, estate planning, and portfolio optimisation strategies. Among the financial planners in this division are a number who write on financial planning strategies for professional publications.

Client Focus

In response to the increasing sophistication of its clients' needs, Ord Minnett has diversified its products and offers clients a one stop shop service. The company has designed structured products to suit clients' borrowing, deposit, and portfolio management needs, not just their share broking execution requirements. The organisation provides for the do-it-yourself investor who requires little advice, as well as for the client who needs more in-depth analysis.

With 13 offices in Australia, Ord Minnett is able to service its very large and very loyal rural, non-metropolitan client base. Rural clients appreciate the traditional nature of the company, the quality of advice provided, and the personal relationships that the company fosters.

Ord Minnett is committed to making contributions to community and charitable organisations by promoting their activities and providing financial support. The company and its staff contribute to the Australian Financial Markets Foundation for Children and are a major corporate sponsor of the United Way, Fred Hollows Foundation, Cancer Council, the Salvation Army's Education Foundation, and other organisations that support the arts.

Building on its long tradition of service in the Australian financial services industry, Ord Minnett will continue to give in-depth, sound advice to its clients into the next millennium.

ORD MINNETT'S CLIENTS RECEIVE PERSONAL, HIGH-QUALITY ADVICE AND SERVICE FROM ITS TEAMS OF ADVISERS. PICTURED HERE ARE (CLOCKWISE FROM TOP LEFT) ROD SKELLET, INSTITUTIONAL OPTIONS DEALER; GEORGIE LOVETT, MANAGER, SECURITIES LENDING; DAVID LEITCH, INDUSTRIAL RESEARCH ANALYST; AND TONY FAY, HEAD OF ORD MINNETT JARDINE FLEMING FUTURES.

FROM LEFT:
HUGH LATIMER IS COMMUNICATIONS MANAGER FOR THE ORD MINNETT GROUP.

AN ORD MINNETT JARDINE FLEMING FUTURES ADVISER CHECKS A MARKET QUOTE FOR A CLIENT.

DAVID JOHNSON (PICTURED RIGHT), ORD MINNETT'S OIL AND GAS RESEARCH ANALYST, VISITS THE CALTEX REFINERY IN SYDNEY.

TAFE NSW

With a history as the oldest and largest vocational education and training institution in Australia, as well as a reputation for flexibility and high standards, TAFE NSW has earned the status of a world leader in its field. Through its pivotal role as an educator in all aspects of commercial and technological activity, TAFE NSW has both contributed to and grown with the development of New South Wales,

Australia's premier state.

TAFE NSW stands for Technical and Further Education New South Wales. The organisation is an integral part of the New South Wales Department of Education and Training. The department delivers education for every age group in the commu-nity, from early childhood, primary and secondary to the vocational training needs of adults. Nearly 420,000 students study each year at TAFE NSW, which delivers 40 per cent of the nation's technical train-ing. TAFE NSW offers more than 1600 courses taught by more than 16,000 teachers, who are drawn from their specialty fields in industry, commerce, management, technol-ogy, and the arts.

TAFE NSW students acquire qualifications that are recognised and used by employers across Australia and internationally.

The organisation's mission is to help students achieve their potential by providing quality education in practical working skills of all kinds, from manual tasks to high-technology fields and management. With cam-puses throughout New South Wales, TAFE NSW provides vocational training in nearly any line of work for which there is a demand, from accounting to zoo keeping.

Instruction is provided using the latest facilities and equipment, and courses vary from a single day's duration to three years of compre-hensive study. TAFE NSW awards qualifications to students who com-plete required course work from certificate up to advanced diploma level. Recognition of relevant work experience and prior learning are recognised by TAFE NSW, to help students complete their qualifications faster. In addition, links with univer-sities provide opportunities for gradu-ating students to move on to higher levels of education if they choose to do so.

A Proud Tradition

The ability to adapt to the changing needs of both employers and students has formed the basis of TAFE NSW's longevity and growth. In 1883, the New South Wales government es-tablished the Board of Technical Education, modelled on the London Guilds Institute. Its mission was "to improve the industrial knowledge

Bringing together the old and the new, TAFE NSW offers courses at more than 130 loca-tions across the state, including this historic site at Liverpool College of TAFE, Sydney (top).

Helping communities to get their rural industries moving is all part of the service at TAFE NSW (bottom).

its innovative Open Training and Education Network (OTEN). Using the World Wide Web, other multimedia resources and the latest advances in delivery systems, OTEN ensures that effective learning services are available to all residents across the expanse of New South Wales (and indeed, Australia), no matter how remote or isolated they might be. OTEN offers flexible delivery systems, including satellite broadcasts, computer-based training, video-conferencing, teleconferencing, and electronic mail.

Training for the
Sydney 2000 Olympic Games
TAFE NSW is especially proud in its appointment as Official Training Services Supporter to the Sydney 2000 Olympic Games. The Olympic Games Training Unit was established in 1998 to support the training of the Olympic and Paralympic Games staff in management, as well as the proposed volunteers who will be the public face of the Sydney 2000 Games. The unit works closely with Sydney Organising Committee for the Olympic Games (SOCOG) in auditing skills needs, and in developing and delivering training programs.

Back to the Future
TAFE NSW continuously develops courses to meet the changing needs of employers and students. All courses are reviewed every three years to reflect current practices in the workplace. The high quality of its practical, professional, and industry-specific training ensures that TAFE NSW will remain a leader in vocational education and training now and in the 21st century.

STUDENTS LEARN THE LATEST TECHNIQUES AND INDUSTRY STANDARDS ON THE JOB AND IN THE CLASSROOM AT TAFE NSW.

FROM THE KITCHENS TO THE COAL FIELDS, TAFE NSW GRADUATES TAKE WITH THEM PRACTICAL SKILLS AND A REPUTATION FOR EXCELLENCE.

of workmen by teaching the sciences and principles underlying their handicrafts." The board assumed management of the Sydney Mechanics' School of Arts Working Men's College, which had been set up five years earlier. It later became known as the Sydney Technical College, popularly referred to as Sydney Tech. From these beginnings, TAFE NSW has today developed into a network of 12 institutes comprising 120 campuses throughout metropolitan Sydney and New South Wales.

TAFE NSW is now the largest educational entity in Australia and one of the largest in the world. The organisation has also built strong relationships with industry and professional bodies on an international scale. One example of TAFE NSW's partnerships in this area is Austraining International, an organisation specialising in worldwide training initiatives.

Working with Industry
The commercial arm of TAFE NSW, known as TAFE PLUS, offers employers consultancy services that draw upon the strength of its vast resources and expertise in training. TAFE PLUS develops courses or modifies existing ones to meet the specific needs of employers across Australia and the world.

Working alongside existing personnel, TAFE PLUS specialists assess workers' levels of competence and skill. The results of these audits are then used to customise training programs that match clients' needs in introducing new procedures, raising standards, and meeting new and higher expectations in the workplace. Companies that have successfully engaged the specialised services of TAFE PLUS range from small businesses to large multinationals.

Distance Education
TAFE NSW has established itself as a leader in distance learning through

THE VISION THAT GUIDES AUSTRALIAN BUSINESS LIMITED IS the goal of championing the development, capability, and prosperity of Australian industry. The organisation has a long and successful history of effecting significant policy developments: The alliances it has forged have led Australian Business to occupy a pivotal position in the economic life of the nation. ∞ As a business improvement resource group,

PHILIP HOLT (LEFT), MANAGING DIRECTOR OF AUSTRALIAN BUSINESS, IS PICTURED HERE WITH THE HONOURABLE JOHN HOWARD, MP, PRIME MINISTER OF AUSTRALIA.

Australian Business offers services that help its members improve their businesses. In describing Australian Business, members of the organisation say it is one they can trust, and one that adds value to their business.

The organisation lobbies government and regulatory bodies, whose decisions affect the wellbeing of members' businesses. Its policy unit operates through a number of committees whose main policy topics include taxation, occupational health and safety, and environmental and industrial policy.

The policy unit encourages members to raise any matters of concern for research, investigation, and analysis. As a key national economic and policy institution, the unit has prepared significant submissions that have influenced national business policy in major areas of concern to the business community, such as taxation, employment, and industry development.

Unified Approach

Australian Business' members incorporate a broad cross-section of industry. The organisation represents small, medium, and large businesses that operate in rural and metropolitan areas.

The organisation tailors cost-effective solutions for members to help their businesses grow and succeed. It offers an integrated service that draws expertise from eight complementary, core service groups: Business Improvement, Workplace Management, Occupational Health and Safety, Learning and Skills Development, International Trade, Health Services, Information and Online, and Labour Market and Recruitment.

In recent years, the organisation's staff has doubled, reflecting the increasing depth and breadth of expertise that Australian Business is constantly developing. Part of this development has been the implementation of a national electronic network called ChamberNet as part of its electronic communications strategy. For the first time in Australian history, the chambers of commerce and their members across Australia are linked, pooling their collective knowledge and information.

At the Cutting Edge

The organisation's Web site (http://www.abol.net) encourages the exchange of information within the network and throughout the world, offering market intelligence, trade facts, databases, and news and current affairs.

Australian Business has also developed Showcase and TradeHub as other online services. The Showcase facility displays information about members' services and products on an electronic catalogue. Each member's presence on the catalogue can be made into a Web page at a competitive cost, enabling members to attract more traffic to their businesses.

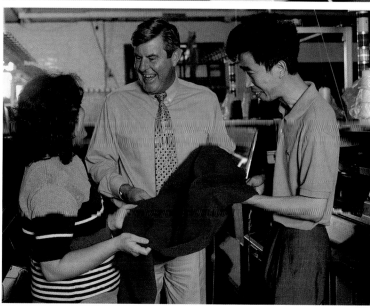

As a cutting-edge electronic commerce system, TradeHub is constantly developing to improve business opportunities for Australian Business' members. It provides a facility for posting and replying to requests for information or for quotations. The electronic data interchange system transmits orders to suppliers via fax and the Internet. It also provides invoicing and payment systems.

Australian Business Foundation

The Australian Business Foundation was initiated by Australian Business, and aims to address essential issues that confront businesses and that affect their future development, Australia's international competitiveness, and job-generation capability.

The foundation is an independent body with its own board, personnel, and budget. Its research is political and designed to challenge

convention through the commission and publication of a number of research studies. The foundation also sponsors conferences and briefings.

To the Future

As a major innovator, Australian Business provides businesses with practical and powerful business solutions. Teams of highly qualified and experienced business professionals provide expert advice on business-, management-, and employer-related issues in a concerted effort to see Australian business grow in the new millennium.

AUSTRALIAN BUSINESS MEMBER COMPANIES INCLUDE REAL FOODS PTY LTD (TOP LEFT AND RIGHT), CALCOUP INC. PTY LTD (MIDDLE LEFT AND RIGHT), AND ROTTERBUILT FURNITURE PTY LTD (BOTTOM).

COMMITTED TO A DISTINCTIVE HEALTH AND HEALING MINISTRY throughout its history, Sydney Adventist Hospital (SAH) maintains a pre-eminent position today as a cutting-edge health care institution. "Sydney Adventist Hospital is committed to total restoration of the body, mind, and spirit for those who seek our services," says Ian Grice, the Hospital's chief executive officer. "Our values of compas-

sion, integrity, professionalism, service, and trust are the foundation of our pursuit of excellence."

With a 324-bed capacity, SAH is the largest private hospital in the state of New South Wales and was the first in the state to be accredited by the Australian Council on Health Care Standards. The Hospital is the flagship facility in the South Pacific for the worldwide Adventist health care system, which consists of 346 clinics and 163 hospitals in 68 coun-

tries and employs 56,000 people. SAH's 2,000 dedicated staff members and 540 accredited medical practitioners attend to more than 13,000 surgical patients, 24,000 in-patients, and 120,000 outpatients each year, who come from all parts of Australia to receive specialist care and special attention.

SAH is committed to patients, its staff, and the community. In taking a holistic approach to the physical, emotional, and spiritual health of each patient, the Hospital affirms

the worth and dignity of the individual. SAH seeks to encourage and assist staff members in attaining the highest standards of excellence, making optimal use of resources and technology. In addition, the Hospital aims to educate the wider community in the principles of healthy living and disease prevention.

SAH's philosophy has remained unchanged throughout the years, and reflects the ideals and practices of the Seventh-Day Adventist Church,

SYDNEY ADVENTIST HOSPITAL WAS ESTABLISHED IN 1903 AND IS THE LARGEST PRIVATE HOSPITAL IN NEW SOUTH WALES WITH 324 BEDS.

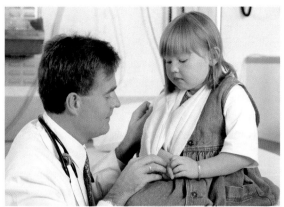
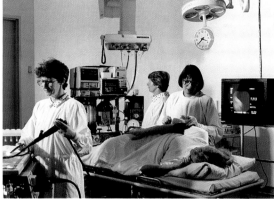
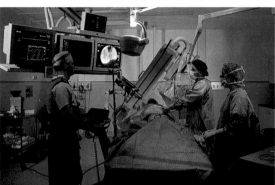
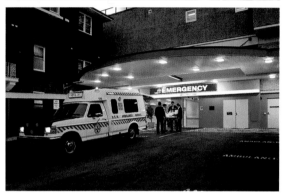

CLOCKWISE FROM TOP LEFT:
THE HOSPITAL OPENED ITS REFUR-
BISHED CHILDREN'S WARD IN 1997. IT
HAS A BED CAPACITY OF 18, INCLUDING
TWO SINGLE ISOLATION ROOMS.

IN 1995, THE HOSPITAL EXPANDED
ITS DAY SURGERY AND ENDOSCOPY
FACILITIES TO IMPROVE CONVENIENCE
FOR PATIENTS.

THE HOSPITAL'S EMERGENCY CARE
DEPARTMENT SEES APPROXIMATELY
18,000 PATIENTS EACH YEAR.

THE HOSPITAL'S CARDIAC CATHETERI-
SATION LABORATORY PROVIDES SPE-
CIALISTS WITH USEFUL TOOLS IN
DIAGNOSING AND RECTIFYING SOME
ABNORMALITIES OF THE HEART.

which owns and manages the not-for-profit hospital, SAH's mission vision, and values statement were aptly summarised in a prayer of dedication written by A.L. King for the opening of a new wing of the Hospital in 1920: "Let us pray that the Lord will bestow upon physicians, managers, and nurses much of his Spirit and blessing: guiding and superintending the institution, and making it all that he has intended in bringing blessing to sick and suffering humanity and glory to his own name."

A Long History

SAH is located on Fox Valley Road, Wahroonga, a suburb on the leafy North Shore, the highest elevation of the Sydney metropolitan area. When the Hospital first opened on January 1, 1903, it was known as the Sydney Sanitarium and Hospital. This facility was later known and today is still often referred to as The San.

Ellen White, a widely published author and a prophet of the Seventh-Day Adventist Church, wanted to establish a campaign of health reform in Australia. Recognised for her great insight into healthy practices, she and fellow Adventists had begun a similar reform program in the United States. Her philosophy on disease prevention and her commitment to

a regimen that included a good diet, fresh air, sunlight, and exercise were revolutionary for the turn of the century.

When she came to Australia, White recommended that the church build its own permanent facilities, with one in Sydney to accommodate at least 100 patients. A site of 220 hectares of bushland was selected at what was then a fair distance from the metropolis. Some 79 hectares were devoted to the Hospital, and the remainder were used to house administrative and

other service buildings, including Sanitarium Health Foods. The land was also used for growing vegetables for the patients' meals, and the Hospital kept a dairy herd for its milk supply.

With an original cost of A£2,300, the land is now valued at $400 million. Dr. Merritt Kellogg, the brother of Kellogg's Corn Flakes inventor John Harvey Kellogg, designed the first hospital. It was a wooden structure, costing a very modest A£8,000 and built largely by volunteer labour.

SYDNEY ADVENTIST HOSPITAL OFFERS
VEGETARIAN CUISINE AND LAUNCHED
ITS NEW INTERNATIONAL MENU IN
MARCH 1998.

Changing with the Times

SAH's progress over the years has been marked by many milestones. In 1915, Bethel, a maternity cottage, was opened for mothers and babies. A disaster was averted in 1919, when a major fire broke out and threatened the Hospital's main building. Fortunately, the staff had contained the fire by the time the local fire brigade arrived, and only the tower, the operating theatre, and some nurses' accommodations were destroyed.

THE HOSPITAL PRIDES ITSELF ON ITS HIGH STANDARD OF CARE (LEFT).

THE THEATRE COMPLEX HAS 10 OPERATING SUITES WITH TWO DEDICATED TO CARDIOTHORACIC SURGERY (RIGHT).

The prestige of the Hospital was enhanced in 1927, when the Nurses' Training School was granted official state registration. Today, SAH is an affiliated teaching hospital of the University of Sydney, and the Avondale College School of Nursing is located on campus.

New wings with new treatment rooms and maternity wards were added in 1933, and the facade was modernised with a portico added in 1936. During the World War II years, the institution came close to being commandeered by the US Army, but the Hospital's identity was preserved. New operating theatres were completed in 1944, and a nurses' residence was constructed in 1952. In the decade that followed, a men's residence was built, and additions were made to the service blocks to include kitchen amenities, classrooms, and a laboratory. The year 1971 marked the beginning of a major construction program that included the Fox Valley Medical and Dental Centre, the School of Nursing, and Wahroonga Activities Centre.

On June 10, 1973, when the present 10-storey hospital was opened, its name was changed to Sydney Adventist Hospital to embrace the name of the church and to clarify the nature of the work of the Hospital. The word "sanitarium" has different connotations in Australia than in America,

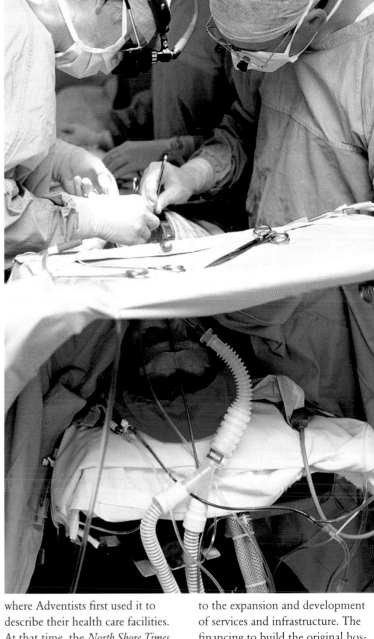

where Adventists first used it to describe their health care facilities. At that time, the *North Shore Times*, the local newspaper, reported, "Every effort has been made by the Hospital to re-create in the new building the atmosphere of friendliness and warmth which always characterised the old Sydney Sanitarium and Hospital."

Fundraising Provides Needed Services

Throughout SAH's history, fundraising has contributed significantly to the expansion and development of services and infrastructure. The financing to build the original hospital was raised by the church's Australasian Medical Missionary and Benevolent Association from voluntary donations. Currently, hundreds of thousands of dollars are raised each year by the Hospital's snack bar operation alone, which is staffed by volunteers.

Jacaranda Lodge is one beneficiary of fundraising activities. It offers low-cost accommodation—a home away from home—for families of patients undergoing critical care. Having 28 rooms equipped with twin beds and four communal kitchens, Jacaranda Lodge is located within the grounds of SAH. The Cancer Support Centre, founded in 1993, is located at the front of Jacaranda Lodge and offers free counselling and support.

State-of-the-Art Treatment

The development of Jacaranda Lodge exemplifies SAH's commitment to improving services and the comfort of patients. Its commitment to making optimal use of resources is reflected in the skillful adoption of the latest high-tech medical procedures. All of the Hospital's medical, diagnostic, and therapeutic services are conveniently located under one roof. There are 10 state-of-the-art operating theatre suites for a wide range of surgical procedures, including two fully equipped designated cardiothoracic theatres. Surgical disciplines include cardiac, orthopaedic, urology, plastic and reconstructive, oral and dental, and ophthalmology. Among the most common types of surgery performed are open and closed-heart surgery, and hip, knee, and shoulder replacements.

A homelike atmosphere has been created in the Hospital's 50-bed maternity wing, and some 2,600 babies are born in the delivery suites each year. Included is a special care nursery to look after premature babies and newborns requiring specialist medical attention.

Use of the ambulatory day surgery unit, completed in 1995, is rapidly growing. The Emergency Care Department was established in response to the local community's needs, and in its first year of operation, 18,000

patients were served. It was the first emergency department opened in a private hospital on Sydney's north shore.

The Paediatric Department, which was refurbished in 1997, gives children the opportunity to take an orientation tour to help them prepare for surgery. To assist a speedy recovery, parents are encouraged to stay with their children in the children's ward, even overnight.

SAH's Heart Care program is one of the most respected in Australia. In-patients and outpatients are provided with comprehensive care, with specialists present in the intensive and coronary units by day, and on call by night. The Cardiac Rehabilitation program educates patients to better cope with heart disease following discharge.

In its commitment to promoting healthy lifestyles, SAH serves vegetarian meals with an international flavour from Italy, Thailand, India, and Mexico. Both patients and staff enjoy five-star vegetarian cuisine. The kitchen will also satisfy patients' special requests, including meat or chicken.

Spreading the Care

SAH's commitment to health care reaches beyond Australia's shores with a program that began in 1986 as Operation Open Heart, in which

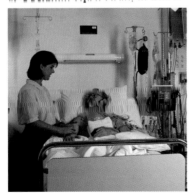

a complete, fully equipped volunteer cardiac surgical team travels to developing countries. Today, the program includes plastic surgery. Now called Health Care Outreach, it sends teams of volunteers—who pay their own travel expenses—to countries including Papua New Guinea, Fiji, Vanuatu, Nepal, China, Mongolia, and Solomon Islands.

Closer to home, SAH has developed a harmonious relationship with its community by inviting local people to open days and special family days. The annual Carols by Candlelight, which has been held for more than 30 years, attracts some 5,000 people.

As SAH assesses health care needs, it plans programs accordingly. For example, a home health care program was recently created because hospital stays were becoming shorter. Administratively, the Hospital revamped its structure so that the care of patients is approached as one sequence of events rather than separate episodes of care. SAH continually strives to improve its programs and procedures.

The founders of SAH were men and women of great faith in God, in his compassion, and in his ability to bring relief and hope through cooperation of human effort and divine power. Sydney Adventist Hospital stands as testimony to this belief and practice.

From the very beginning, St Vincent's Private Hospital earned a reputation for setting high standards in the health care service industry. It has become one of Australia's major private hospitals, its name synonymous with excellence. ∞ The Sisters of Charity, an order of Catholic nuns, opened St Vincent's Private Hospital on its current site in 1909. Centrally located on the fringe of the Sydney Central

Business District in Darlinghurst, St Vincent's Private Hospital is a 230-bed acute medical and surgical hospital providing services across all major specialities. It is the flagship of the 20 facilities that form the Sisters of Charity Health Service, the largest private health care provider in Australia.

As a not-for-profit institution that is not funded by government, St Vincent's Private Hospital proudly claims its Independence to provide services that it identifies as necessary to fulfil its mission of caring within a Catholic tradition. Surplus funds go to the development and maintenance of programs that support important community projects. The outreach work of the sisters includes the providing of crisis accommodation, support programs for young mothers, court support, and a counselling service for rural families.

Success

Patients in surveys have rated St Vincent's Private Hospital as the number one hospital in Australia and the institution's nursing care as outstanding. In addition, the surveys of many health insurance companies reveal a high level of satisfaction among St Vincent's Private Hospital's patients, as well as excellent clinical outcomes.

The success of the hospital is clearly demonstrated by the increasing number of admissions, from 9,000 patients to more than 14,000 per year over the course of the past decade. Only the size of the hospital has limited its growth.

History

A mission of care has been at the core of the work of the Sisters of Charity since their arrival in Australia in 1838. To look after the indigent ill, the sisters opened St Vincent's Hospital, the first Catholic hospital in Australia, in 1857 at Potts Point. It was financed through voluntary subscriptions and fundraising activities. In 1870, with further financial assistance from supporters, the sisters built the first St Vincent's Hospital at its current site at Darlinghurst.

As the colony grew, the number of people who wanted and could afford a private room increased. The sisters saw this as the opportunity to continue their work by using the fees from private patients to subsidise the hospital's running costs and expansion.

In 1908, a building that had housed a hospice became available, and the sisters established St Vincent's Private Hospital there. Expanding steadily by adding new medical technology and advanced electronic equipment for patient care, St Vincent's Private Hospital outgrew its quarters. To meet the challenges, a new hospital was built, and in 1977, Cardinal Freeman opened and blessed the

St Vincent's Private Hospital is centrally located in Darlinghurst, New South Wales. The hospital is easily accessible by all forms of transport (left).

Dr Phil Stricker (right) undertakes a medical procedure. The hospital has five fully equipped operating rooms in the main theatre suite (right).

DAVID DARE PARKER, WILDLIGHT

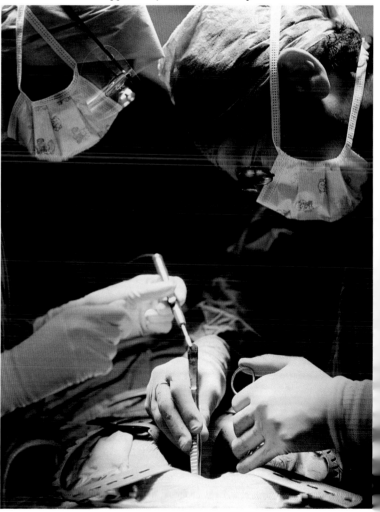

CLOCKWISE FROM TOP:
NURSE BRONWYN AXE (LEFT) ATTENDS
VALERIE DIAMOND DURING HER STAY
AT ST VINCENT'S PRIVATE HOSPITAL.
PATIENTS IN SURVEYS HAVE RATED ST
VINCENT'S PRIVATE HOSPITAL AS THE
NUMBER ONE HOSPITAL IN AUSTRALIA
AND THE INSTITUTION'S NURSING
CARE AS OUTSTANDING.

THE HIGH CLINICAL STANDARDS, DEDI-
CATION TO THE CARE OF THE PATIENT
AS AN INDIVIDUAL, AND CENTRAL
LOCATION OF ST VINCENT'S PRIVATE
HOSPITAL HAVE EARNED IT A REPUTA-
TION THAT PUTS IT AT THE APEX OF
AUSTRALIA'S HEALTH CARE SYSTEM.

CHEF BILL LYMBEROPOULOS IS ONE
OF MANY HIGHLY PROFESSIONAL AND
DEDICATED STAFF MEMBERS AT ST
VINCENT'S PRIVATE HOSPITAL.

new acute medical and surgical private hospital.

Christian Values Maintained

The sisters have devolved management and strategic direction of the hospital to a lay executive, while maintaining the Sisters of Charity's goal of bringing the healing ministry of Christ to those in their care. Embodied in the mission of the hospital are the core values that are the foundation of the sisters' mission: compassion, justice, respect for human dignity, commitment to excellence, and unity founded on harmony and collaboration.

The pastoral care team, which consists of ministers from all denominations, is available at all times to provide emotional and spiritual support to patients. Although the private hospital is a Catholic institution, there is no religious prerequisite for staff, patients, or any other relationship that the hospital may develop.

Technology

St Vincent's Private Hospital invests heavily in acquiring cutting-edge technology to constantly improve its ability to provide patients with a superior quality of service and care. New investigative technology often obviates the need for major surgical procedures. This benefits both the patient, who has a shorter hospital stay, and the hospital, as more patients are able to be treated.

The hospital has five fully equipped operating rooms in the main theatre

▶◀ DAVID PRE PARKER, WILDLIGHT

suite, as well as a 12-bed intensive care unit with the latest technological equipment. In addition to general medicine and general surgery, other major clinical services include bone marrow transplantation, cardiology and cardiac investigations, plastic surgery, orthopaedic surgery, and neurosurgery.

The Day Surgery Unit consists of four operating theatres and a dedicated recovery area. This unit provides the maximum care with minimal interruption to patients' lives. To keep abreast of the latest medical developments, the hospital sponsors international conferences, as well as a host of educational forums and seminars for doctors and nurses.

Central

An important feature of the hospital's location is its central position and

accessibility by all forms of transport. Forty percent of patients come from the city's Central Business District and the adjacent eastern suburbs metropolitan region. The remainder come from all corners of the state and nation, and a small but significant number come from overseas.

The driving force of St Vincent's Private Hospital is to provide a Christian health care environment. The high clinical standards, dedication to the care of the patient as an individual, and central location of St Vincent's Private Hospital have earned it a reputation that puts it at the apex of Australia's health care system. With plans to expand the hospital and its ongoing commitment to improving all facets of its services, St Vincent's Private Hospital will continue to attract patients from across Australia and around the world.

GRACE REMOVALS GROUP WAS ESTABLISHED IN 1911 WHEN brothers Albert and Joseph Grace saw an opportunity to diversify their existing business. Nearly three decades before, in 1884, the twosome had begun nurturing a retail business focused on selling and delivering furniture and household items. The original store, located in the centre of Sydney, quickly forged an excellent reputation, and customers began

asking for assistance when moving house.

In hopes of building on the momentum they had already established, Albert and Joseph purchased the assets of a small New South Wales removals company. With little more than a team of horses, two carts, and a storage repository, the brothers were well positioned to make their new business flourish.

Today, Grace Removals is Australia's largest removals company, with more than 50 branches throughout Australia and New Zealand, and a fleet of more than 600 vehicles of varying types and capacities. Grace will move anything anywhere—whether it's across the street or across the world—using the combined resources of rail, road, sea, and air. No matter the scope of a job, the company's vision is to be the most innovative mover and the preferred supplier to companies and organisations.

International Horizons

Working on the sound business principles of quality, service, and value, Grace Removals grew rapidly

from its inception, maintaining profitability even throughout two world wars and the Great Depression. By 1946, the company had grown to 52 employees and 20 vehicles.

Beginning in 1950, the company pursued a growth strategy centred on acquisitions and branch openings beyond its home base in Sydney, progressively forming a national network. By 1967, Grace had become the first removals company in Australia to offer coverage of the entire continent. In the years that followed, the company moved onto the global stage, taking its prestigious position as one of the largest international removals organisations in the world.

A Recipe for Success

For Grace Removals, ongoing growth and prosperity can be linked to a strong work force and a dedication

to innovative services. Because the company values its staff as its primary resource, Grace has planned and implemented a rigorous regimen of training throughout its operations and locations. "We've been dedicated to training since the inception of the business," says Peter Harden, national sales and marketing manager. "Our people are taught how to lift, carry, and pack. This way, we are assured that our quality standards are uniformly maintained throughout the business. This is one of Grace's strengths."

The company has also been careful to tailor its services to the specific needs of its household and corporate customers. Grace will store household goods and business documents, relocate entire companies, and transport everything from cars and boats to house plants and the family pet.

THE HEADQUARTERS FOR GRACE REMOVALS GROUP IS CONVENIENTLY LOCATED ADJACENT TO THE M2 MOTORWAY (LEFT).

GRACE REMOVALS GROUP ENSURES PROFESSIONAL WRAPPING AND PACKING TO THE HIGHEST STANDARD (RIGHT).

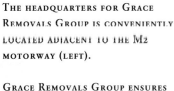

In 1985, the company brought its expertise in planning to bear when it introduced the Grace Action-Pac, an information kit to assist household customers with their relocation. "With our many years of experience, we acknowledge there is a personal side to moving," says Harden. "The Grace Action-Pac provides a variety of items to make the transition to a new home easier, including electoral advice cards, change of address cards, and a planner and check list."

The company developed its Grace Valet service in response to the needs of people who must hit the ground running after a relocation. Grace's valet staff helps clients establish a workable and ordered home quickly after a move, whether it involves making the beds, putting away clothes, setting up the kitchen, or handling countless other tasks necessary to make the relocation a smooth one. Complimentary fresh flowers are also a thoughtful touch.

For business customers, Grace offers a one stop solution. The company can provide cataloguing and packing services, storage and retrieval, archive supplies, and security destruction. What's more, Grace carries out business moves 24 hours a day, seven days a week to ensure minimal disruption.

The company is especially proud of Grace Fine Art, a highly specialised service that handles and transports paintings, ceramics, antiques, and other valuable articles. Leading art galleries and collectors have come to rely on Grace to transport their fine works of art.

A Good Corporate Citizen

Over the years, Grace has made an effort to apply its removals expertise to community needs. This commitment is evident in the company's sponsorship of many community activities, as well as its rapid response with equipment and assistance in times of emergency and natural disaster.

Grace is also a major sponsor of Artexpress, serving as official carrier for all moves within Australia. This travelling exhibition consists of selected works submitted by New South Wales students for the visual arts examination of the Higher School Certificate. Since its inception in the 1980s, the program has steadily gained a worldwide reputation and has even been exhibited internationally.

"Artexpress represents a way for us to put something back into the community. We see it as an opportunity to use our expertise in fine art to help young people in their creative endeavours," says Harden.

Building on a strong foundation, Grace Removals plans to continue developing innovative services that respond to changing needs, while providing unsurpassed value to its household and business customers. The company's reputation as an industry pioneer has afforded it a competitive edge throughout its history of expansion, as it surely will in the future.

CLOCKWISE FROM TOP:
THE GRACE CUSTOMER SERVICE CENTER IS LOCATED AT SEVEN HILLS.

THIS STORAGE AND DISTRIBUTION FACILITY IS PART OF GRACE'S OPERATIONS.

ARTWORK RECEIVES SPECIAL ATTENTION FROM GRACE PROFESSIONALS.

AUSTRALIA'S FIRST COMMERCIAL RADIO STATION, RADIO 2UE has been Sydney's premier radio station since beaming its first broadcast on Australia Day in 1925. With integrity, honesty, and respect as its guiding principles, 2UE prides itself on serving the people of Sydney with a format of news, entertainment, and on-air conversation—in addition to supporting old-fashioned community service. Listening to feedback

BREAKFAST RADIO IN SYDNEY IS DOMINATED BY ALAN JONES ON 2UE. A MIXTURE OF ENTERTAINING TALKBACK, HARD-HITTING EDITORIALS, AND TAKE-NO-PRISONERS INTERVIEWS COMBINE WTIH NEWS, TRAFFIC, AND WEATHER REPORTS TO START THE DAY IN SYDNEY (LEFT).

ORIGINATING FROM RADIO 2UE, THE JOHN LAWS MORNING PROGRAM IS SYNDICATED ACROSS AUSTRALIA, AIRING ON SOME 80 STATIONS AND HEARD BY 2 MILLION LOYAL LISTENERS. LAWS ACHIEVED HIS 100TH SURVEY IN THE NUMBER ONE POSITION IN 1998 (RIGHT).

enables the station to identify listeners' needs, and has helped 2UE earn the respect of listeners in Australia's most cosmopolitan city.

"The business has had its ups and downs, but 2UE has been at or near the top for 40 years. If we're not number one, we're usually number two. There have been few exceptions to that," says John Conde, the chairman of the board for the station.

A Colourful History

Famous names that have broadcast on 2UE represent a wide variety of luminaries from the fields of broadcast entertainment and journalism in

Australia. Gary O'Callaghan, Brian Henderson, Bob Rogers, Howard Craven, and Brian White are some of the names that preceded today's on-air line-up of personalities, who attract millions of listeners across the nation in syndicated programs.

2UE was established by Cecil Vincent Stevenson, whose two sons are now directors of the parent company. Stevenson was first granted approval to conduct broadcast transmission tests from his home at Maroubra, in Sydney's eastern suburbs, in 1922. In the next year, authorities introduced sealed-set arrangements, whereby listeners could receive only

one broadcaster's signal on their wireless sets. Without popular support, this scheme failed immediately.

Stevenson received one of the two commercial licences that were granted by the Australian Government under a then-new radio broadcasting licensing system introduced in 1924. Stevenson chose the call letters 2EU, but later changed them to 2UE for ease of pronunciation. The station began broadcasting on a frequency of 293 metres, and its initial programming went on the air between 8 and 10 p.m. each evening.

At first, Stevenson thought to use the station to promote his own

Each year, Australia Day marks the anniversary of 2UE's initial broadcast and founding in 1925. Pictured here is Freda Whittred at the 1999 Australia Day celebrations.

PHILIP QUIRK, WILDLIGHT

business, a company named Electric Utilities (and the inspiration for the station's call letters), but he soon realised the advantage of broadcasting advertising for other businesses. The first commercial advertisement broadcast for another business was for Stevenson's local butcher shop in Maroubra.

The Stevenson family has been involved in the ownership of the station since the beginning, except for a period between 1986 and 1991. The Lamb family, which owns Broadcast Investments Pty Ltd, bought a controlling interest in 1956, holding it except for that same period. Between 1986 and 1991, the station was owned first by businessman Kerry Packer's interests, and subsequently by another businessman, Alan Bond. With the change in ownership in 1991, the station returned to its traditional format, which attracted a large audience.

Continuing Success

With innovative programming, 2UE was an industry leader in radio's heyday, and marked its position with a number of firsts. For example, in 1928, 2UE broadcast a three-hour concert from the Sydney Town Hall to bid farewell to Italian grand opera artists who were visiting the city—thus beaming the first live broadcast of opera in Australia. Also, to provide

accurate time signals, 2UE purchased a grandfather clock and placed a special microphone in it that would transmit the chimes. Later, the 2UE engineers designed an intricate device that enabled the station to automatically include observatory time signals in the station's transmissions.

In its early years, the station was at the forefront of technological developments. From various locations—including St Mary's Cathedral—the station broadcast the complete proceedings of the Catholic Church's Eucharistic Congress held in Sydney in 1929. In addition, 2UE was among the first radio stations to introduce the machine-gun microphone, which excluded surrounding noise as it picked up a distant sound.

2UE met the challenge of television, responding with programming and a host of personalities, and emerged as the dominant force in broadcasting. The programming format included the introduction of the Top 40, as well as Gary O'Callaghan's breakfast show featuring Sammy Sparrow, the little bird whose chirpy voice sent many children off to school with happy dispositions. O'Callaghan reigned as Sydney's top-rated breakfast announcer for 28 years. Today, breakfast radio in Sydney remains dominated by 2UE, with the former

Rugby Union coach and former speech writer for an Australian prime minister, Alan Jones, who turned talk-show host. An Oxford graduate, Jones has been described as the "indefatigable champion of the individual".

The John Laws morning program is syndicated across Australia, airing on some 80 stations and heard by 2 million loyal listeners. John Laws achieved his 100th survey in the number one position in 1998. The consummate entertainer, interviewer, salesman, and occasional poet, Laws attracts guests ranging from prime ministers to pop stars, and he often finds himself "in defence of the defenceless" as he helps people with problems.

Effective Sales

In a marketing environment dominated by television, radio station 2UE has proved itself again and again to be a powerful and successful sales tool. "2UE is an excellent vehicle for selling goods and services. People continue to be delighted with the results they get on 2UE," says Conde.

Advertisers on 2UE have successfully sold everything from hammers to motor cars. Of significance for advertisers is the strong purchasing power of the 2UE audience. While 2UE's target audience is primarily aged 40 years and older, the station has many younger listeners. 2UE does not target a socioeconomic group, but aims to appeal to a broad cross-section of people, offering different programs to appeal to different audiences and demographics. Advertisers can tailor commercial content by location in syndicated programs. The station can broadcast a single commercial across participating stations simultaneously, or arrange for a mix of advertisements on diverse stations.

News and Entertainment

Programming content on 2UE is driven by the philosophy of keeping people both entertained and informed. When important events happen, people turn to 2UE's recognised, authoritative news service. 2UE's news and its role in broadcasting information during emergencies—such as bush fires—have been acknowledged by awards made to the station and its staff.

A feature of the newsroom has been the development of a manual to enhance and help maintain high standards. The newsroom employs a mix of experienced personnel and cadets with enthusiasm and the desire to be the best. "The expectation is that staff will try to raise standards. That's been a hallmark of 2UE for decades. It's the reason the station enjoys the regard that it does. People know we try to do the right thing," says Conde.

The 2UE newsroom has bureaus located in the state and national parliament houses, and specialist staff members are assigned to cover police and other news sectors. The exceptional quality of the station's news programming reflects the expertise of its reporters.

Over the years, 2UE has also developed good relations with other media outlets. The station has a good rapport with other talk radio stations in other state capital cities, including 3AW in Melbourne, 4BC in Brisbane, 5AA in Adelaide, and 6PR in Perth. For many years, 2UE has been the local distributor for CBS Radio news. In more recent years, the station has established associations with the US networks ABC and CNN.

2UE supplies programming to some 130 stations around the nation through the news and programming service Sky Broadcasting Network, owned by the same parent company. Half of Sky's content is contributed from 2UE.

Sound Corporate Citizen

In its commitment to supporting community activity, 2UE goes the extra mile, giving away more than $500,000 worth of airtime each year. In addition to prerecorded public service announcements, station personalities often read live on-air announcements during programs to benefit community organisations and activities.

Listeners often call in with news of community and charitable activities that the station broadcasts in prime time. Both the station and its staff have received Australian and international awards recognising the station's community service. "We all feel proud when, for instance, we do something that benefits the Children's Hospital. It's an amazing experience to see how these little kids can be assisted and to know that the radio station is helping them," says Conde.

Olympic and Sporting Spirit

2UE has led the field in developing sports broadcasting over the decades. The station's involvement with the Olympics is typical of its sporting spirit. Since the 1950s, 2UE has shared with the Australian Broadcasting Corporation (ABC), the national broadcaster, the opportunity to broadcast the Olympic games in Australia. 2UE has had the exclusive rights for commercial radio, and ABC the rights for noncommercial radio.

ALWAYS A REFLECTION OF SYDNEY'S LIFESTYLE AND CULTURE, 2UE HAS ITSELF BECOME AN IMPORTANT PART OF THE FABRIC OF LIFE IN AUSTRALIA'S LARGEST CITY.

PHILIP QUIRK, WILDLIGHT

2UE's highlight in Olympic broadcasting has been its commitment to the Sydney 2000 Games; the station has signed up as a designated supporter sponsor, and committed itself heavily to supporting the volunteers program. "We feel that we added something extra as part of the Sydney Games," says Conde.

In another sporting arena, 2UE was the first commercial station in the Southern Hemisphere to broadcast horse racing calls. The broadcast featured Lachie Melville, one of the world's first race callers. Race caller Ken Howard was a household name for many years in Sydney.

The 2UE "phantom" description of the important bout between Vic Patrick and Tommy Burns in 1946 is recorded in the annals of Australian broadcasting. When fight organisers refused to grant the station permission to call the fight live from the ringside, 2UE staffers made detailed notes about the progress of the fight, and took them to the fight caller, Clif Cary, whose phantom description was widely acclaimed when publicly acknowledged. More recently, the station's cricket commentaries, coverage of various codes of football, and sports news reporting have marked its continuing commitment to sports broadcasting, earning 2UE a high level of popularity among sporting fans.

Looking Ahead

2UE looks forward to taking advantage of the opportunities that will flow from technological changes that are planned by the broadcasting industry regulatory authorities. The AM broadcasting signal is increasingly contaminated by man-made noise from computers, new distribution cables, lines on poles, and similar sources. New technologies such as digital broadcasting will offer better technical standards and opportunities to develop new services. 2UE will embrace these new technologies and continue to be an innovator in radio broadcasting in Sydney.

Always a reflection of Sydney's lifestyle and culture, 2UE has itself become an important part of the fabric of life in Australia's largest city. With its long tradition of service and innovation, 2UE is sure to be a vital part of the Sydney community for many years to come.

THE BUSINESS HAS HAD ITS UPS AND DOWNS, BUT 2UE HAS BEEN AT OR NEAR THE TOP FOR 40 YEARS," SAYS JOHN CONDE, CHAIRMAN OF THE BOARD FOR THE STATION (TOP).

IN ITS COMMITMENT TO SUPPORTING COMMUNITY ACTIVITY, 2UE GOES THE EXTRA MILE, GIVING AWAY MORE THAN $500,000 WORTH OF AIRTIME EACH YEAR (BOTTOM).

*I*N 1925, THOMAS HUGHES, A SYDNEY BUSINESSMAN, SEIZED the opportunity to introduce into Australia a new technology. John Evans Cornell of the Bates Valve Company of Chicago had developed a revolutionary, multiple-wall paper sack that changed forever the way goods are packaged. Hughes entered into a licensing agreement with the Chicago company and founded Bates Australia as a joint venture.

Now known as Amcor St. Regis Bates (previously St. Regis-ACI), the company's 300 employees operate out of six locations in Australia and one in Singapore. It is a division of Amcor, one of the world's leading integrated packaging and paper companies, with an annual turnover in excess of $6 billion.

The Specialist

"The concept of the multiwall sack might be mature, but by exploring with customers new and innovative ways to use the experience gained, we have been able to deliver real value for mutual benefit," says Brian McConachie, the divisional general manager. With a wide range of customers, Amcor St. Regis Bates is the major supplier of multiwall sacks in Australia, producing principally a multilayer paper, or a paper-film, paper-laminate, or paper-foil product. Some of the biggest customers the division has are major food companies packing products such as flour, sugar, pet food, and milk powder, plus the traditional industrial sector companies packing such items as cement, limestone, and pigments.

Quality accredited to AS9002, Amcor St. Regis Bates' Sydney plant is also the head office for the group,

and home for the equipment and bulk bag operations. Combined with multiwall sacks, these operations enable complete solutions to be offered to satisfy customer needs— "whether it involves designing and commissioning automatic filling systems; tailoring multiwall sacks for specific needs for protection of goods against moisture or loss of aroma and flavour, using latest sealing technology; or providing one-tonne bulk bags," says McConachie.

Part of Sydney

With its long history in Sydney, Amcor St. Regis Bates is proud of the employment opportunities it has provided to Sydneysiders. Its work force reflects the strengths and rich diversity of Sydney's multicultural society. The company has always been committed to upholding high standards in occupational health and safety, and has developed and implemented an in-house training program for its employees. "At Amcor St. Regis Bates, we have a nil injuries policy, and the health and wellbeing of employees are paramount," says McConachie.

The company predicts that it will continue to grow steadily in the future, bringing an increase in local production. Exports will continue to be an important growth factor. Amcor St. Regis Bates will maintain its industry leadership by remaining abreast of new developments in the industry through international licensing arrangements with firms in the United States and Europe. Above all, Amcor St. Regis Bates sees that its future growth will be linked to continued efforts to offer better and smarter solutions to its customers at a competitive cost, while maintaining world-class production quality using the latest technology.

AMCOR ST. REGIS BATES WILL MAINTAIN ITS INDUSTRY LEADERSHIP BY REMAINING ABREAST OF NEW DEVELOPMENTS IN THE INDUSTRY THROUGH INTERNATIONAL LICENSING ARRANGEMENTS WITH FIRMS IN THE UNITED STATES AND EUROPE.

WITH ITS LONG HISTORY IN SYDNEY, AMCOR ST. REGIS BATES IS PROUD OF THE EMPLOYMENT OPPORTUNITIES IT HAS PROVIDED TO SYDNEYSIDERS.

BOEING AUSTRALIA LIMITED IS A LEADING HIGH-TECHNOLOGY aerospace and defence company specialising in design, development, manufacture, installation, and support of key defence systems. Established in Australia for more than 60 years, and with 1,800 employees at facilities throughout the country, Boeing also manufactures complex aerostructure components for export to the world's

leading aircraft companies. Boeing Australia Limited is part of the Boeing Corporation, which employs more than 225,000 people and has total worldwide sales in excess of US$48 billion.

The Boeing Corporation

In 1997, two aviation giants—the Boeing Company and McDonnell Douglas—merged to form the world's largest aerospace company. Today's Boeing is a global enterprise that designs, produces, and supports jetliners and jet fighters, military transports, helicopters, business jets, missiles, rockets, and space-faring vehicles. Having customers in 145 countries and operations in 27 US states, the company ranks among the top 15 Fortune 500 companies.

Boeing is the world's largest military aircraft manufacturer. Among projects currently being undertaken by Boeing Australia are the High Frequency Modernisation project, designed to place all Australian Defence Forces users on a common communications network; an Avionics Upgrade Program for Australia's fleet of F/RF-III strike aircraft that takes the aircraft avionics from analog to digital; integrating the combat and communications systems on the Royal Australia Navy fleet of Collins Class submarines; operation of a number of communication bases across Australia; and the operation of a helicopter training school.

For more than 30 years, Boeing has been the world's leader in commercial flight. More than 9,000 of its jetliners are in service worldwide, and market projections show a demand for 16,000 new passenger jets over the next 20 years. Boeing will compete in this market with a flexible

family of jetliners ranging from its newest—the 717, 777, and Next Generation 737—to its 747, 757, and 767 aircraft, offering airline customers a wide choice of payload and range options with superior operating economics.

Beyond the Space Frontier

As the leading contractor for the US National Aeronautics and Space Administration (NASA), Boeing is linked to the future exploration and burgeoning commercial use of outer space. It is the prime contractor on the International Space Station, and provides systems integration, operations support, and payload preparation for space shuttles. Boeing has teamed with Teledesic Corporation to create a satellite network that will provide an "Internet in the sky." Sea Launch—a joint venture with Norway, Russia, and the Ukraine—will put satellites into orbit from a mobile platform in the Pacific Ocean. The company is also developing advanced versions of its highly reliable Delta rocket to provide com-

mercial and military customers with larger, more economical payload launch capabilities.

Boeing has broad, corporatewide initiatives to continuously improve the quality, performance, and affordability of all its products. These initiatives are driven by a commitment to achieve total customer satisfaction, to capitalise on the skills and strengths of a diverse work force, and to be the world-class leader in the aerospace industry.

BOEING AUSTRALIA LIMITED IS A LEADING HIGH-TECHNOLOGY DEFENCE AND AEROSPACE COMPANY WITH RESPONSIBILITY FOR THE INTEGRATION OF THE COMBAT AND COMMUNICATION SYSTEMS ON THE COLLINS CLASS SUBMARINES (TOP).

BOEING IS THE WORLD'S LARGEST MILITARY AIRCRAFT MANUFACTURER, AND BOEING AUSTRALIA HAS UNDERTAKEN A NUMBER OF PROJECTS FOR THE AUSTRALIAN MILITARY (BOTTOM).

THE AMERICAN CHAMBER OF COMMERCE IN AUSTRALIA (AmCham) was established in 1961 by a small group of American and Australian businessmen headed by Ed T. Hamilton and Kevin Bannon, with the encouragement of then US Consul General Frank A. Waring. This small group has grown into a membership of more than 1,800, which consists of a near equal number of Australian and US companies.

TODAY, THE AMERICAN CHAMBER OF COMMERCE IN AUSTRALIA (AMCHAM) IS RECOGNISED AS THE MOST ACTIVE BUSINESS LOBBY AND PROMOTIONAL ORGANISATION IN THE COUNTRY.

Today, AmCham is recognised as the most active business lobby and promotional organisation in Australia.

The Right Time

In earlier days, businessmen with an interest in trade and investment between the United States and Australia regularly met at the American Club, located in Sydney's historic Rocks precinct. Many of the Americans knew one another from the World War II years, when some of them first visited Australia and developed local business connections. The 1960s saw an expanding American business presence and an excellent rapport between Australian and US businessmen. Hamilton was convinced that it was the perfect time to cement business relationships with the creation of an institution to facilitate their growth. Among the founding subscriber companies that paid AmCham's first dues—and which are still members today—are American Express, 3M, NCR, Otis, Pepsi-Cola, AMF, Boeing, Caltex, Ford, Gillette, and Goodyear.

Hamilton initially served as AmCham's presiding officer, and Bannon was the first executive director. Colleen Collinge has been with AmCham from the beginning, joining six months after it was registered. Collinge began as a secretary, and today, she holds the title of deputy general manager of the New South Wales division. Her first memory of the office is a single room containing three desks, seven extension phones, one typewriter, a *Thomas Register of American Manufacturers*, and a "big packing case on the floor full of files."

Presence across Australia

After several relocations to various Sydney office blocks, today AmCham's Sydney office, which is also the national headquarters, is located where its activities began: in the Rocks. While Sydney offers a diversity of environments, the Rocks—located adjacent to the Sydney Harbour Bridge—is historically and architecturally unique. Being close to the Sydney Central Business District (CBD), it offers visitors to AmCham convenient bus and train transport, as well as street parking.

From a single office in Sydney, AmCham has extended its presence and operations across Australia. Apart from the national office, the organisation has regional offices in every mainland state, with Tasmania served through Melbourne.

"Our objectives haven't changed over the years. Our objectives are to promote the interests of American and Australian business, and to promote trade, commerce, and investment between the two countries. We also try to do some worthwhile community work. The way we operate has changed. Our library and communications are now electronic. The chamber is at the leading edge of business communications and business advocacy these days," says CEO Charles W. Blunt.

Government Relations

As an advocate for its members, AmCham lobbies government on any issue that affects the general

business climate, level of investment, and profitability of companies in Australia. The organisation facilitates liaisons with government, furnishes letters of introduction for members, and provides a commercial library, which offers a wealth of trade and commercial information. AmCham's library collection includes directories of US businesses in Australia cross referenced with their products and services. In addition, a register of business consultants has been compiled in-house.

AmCham organises Australia's largest and most diverse business information and events programs, conducting more than 800 events each year. These include luncheon and breakfast seminars, briefings, round-table forums, trade shows, and a variety of activities programs.

As one of 76 similar chambers across the world, AmCham offers members access to a powerful and extensive network of information and assistance. AmCham's staff is experienced and professional, with a lobbying expertise that stems from daily contact with government departments and regulatory authorities. "They know their job, the market, and the members. They're good 'people' people. They regard members as the lifeblood of the organisation. We exist to serve our members, and we think we do it very well," says Blunt.

Community Involvement

A very active community affairs program ensures that the wider community benefits from AmCham's commitment to being an active corporate citizen. For example, AmCham introduced the Young Achievement program to Australia. School students are given the opportunity to experience setting up and managing an enterprise. Students identify a market need for which they develop, produce, and market a product. The program teaches how business contributes to the wealth of a community.

AmCham also established a foundation to operate a program that provides sponsorships for trade union leaders to study at Harvard, in order to gain a broader perspective on their role in the business world and in the community. Each year, AmCham also adopts two charities, usually from among those that support children or other international causes.

The American Chamber of Commerce in Australia is proud of the contribution it has made to the economic relations between the United States and Australia, as well as the personal ties it has helped build between businesspeople. Says Blunt, "There is one organisation speaking with one voice on behalf of American business in Australia. That makes us more effective in our dealings with governments in Canberra and Washington. I think membership will continue to grow because Australia continues to attract US investment."

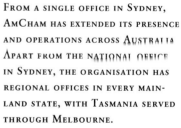

As the Olympic City turns with confidence to the new millennium, CB Richard Ellis will be there, helping Sydney grow to new and sustainable heights. ⁓◇ The world market leader in real estate services, CB Richard Ellis has been a key player in Australian property since 1966. "We're proud of our contribution to Sydney's skyline," says Bill Chillingworth, CB Richard Ellis Chief Operating Officer

"Our clients depend on our distinct abilities to forsee the landscape ahead and how it affects every aspect of their business," says Bill Chillingworth, CB Richard Ellis Chief Operating Officer for Australia and New Zealand (top).

Designed by leading architect Harry Seidler, 9 Castlereagh Street was disposed of by CB Richard Ellis to AMP for $112.75 million (bottom).

for Australia and New Zealand. "We have shared a partnership in growth with our clients here in Sydney and throughout Australia for more than 30 years."

By any number of measures—revenues, transaction volume, employees, and company-owned principal offices—CB Richard Ellis is the largest vertically integrated commercial real estate services company in the world. The company has built its global reputation on providing clients consistent service and excellence no matter where they operate worldwide.

"Here in Sydney, this commitment to excellence is reflected in the strength of experience of the very finest professionals in our business lines," says Chillingworth. "No matter what our clients require, they get simply the best advice and service across our core services portfolio—the best sales and leasing, property management, corporate advisory services and asset services, market research, and property and plant-and-machinery valuations."

Sydney, a city with a highly educated, diverse population, is fast becoming a regional hub for business throughout Asia and the Pacific. Leading property companies are taking a major role in helping find industries the best accommodation mix for their rapidly evolving needs. In recent times, for instance, CB Richard Ellis has found office space for major multinational companies transferring their international customer call centres here, and establishing regional headquarters in Sydney.

Despite its cosmopolitan international outlook, Sydney retains its unique Australian flavour; doing business here may well be a microcosm of navigating the new world of international commerce.

"To paraphrase Oscar Wilde:

Australia and America are two great nations divided by a common language," says Chillingworth. "The challenge for multinational service providers is to talk the language of service excellence, and deliver on that promise, whether they are in Sydney or Los Angeles—or Shanghai."

CB Richard Ellis is the result of a 1998 merger between two unique companies sharing distinctive pasts and a common vision for the future. CB Commercial, North America's largest commercial property firm, and Richard Ellis International, a 200-year-old real estate leader. The new company has the pedigree to meet the global service challenge. "Our business strategy is focused very much on developing fresh market opportunities for our clients based on local knowledge and our unmatched global platform," says Chillingworth.

Headquartered in Los Angeles, with more than 10,000 employees, CB Richard Ellis serves real estate owners, investors, and occupiers through more than 320 principal offices in 30 countries.

In Australia and New Zealand, CB Richard Ellis has more than 500 staff in 14 offices, including three in

New South Wales: North Sydney, Parramatta, and its Australasian headquarters in the heart of Sydney's Central Business District. "We provide clients with services across the realm of property sectors, here in Sydney and around the world—from commercial property to industrial real estate, and from hotels to retail centres," says NSW Senior Managing Director Tom Southern.

"The advantages of scale and global coverage reap rewards for our customers," says Chillingsworth. "With the commoditisation of information, amassed intelligence is now the critical factor. To provide services in a wide geographical scope gives you a true way to serve your client."

The central belief at CB Richard Ellis is that the local business is best run by local people, allowing the company to service cross-border real estate investors with on-the-ground experience and an international network unequalled in the industry. "Our standard is to achieve best-of-class services and property knowledge for all commercial real estate needs," says Chillingworth.

"Our clients depend on our distinct abilities to foresee the landscape ahead and how it affects every aspect of their business—from changing economics, cultures, and technologies to transitions in international markets and communications," says Chillingworth. "By using our strength, resources, and passion, we help our clients navigate the increasingly complex world of real estate decision-making the only way we know how: successfully."

Mᴀɴᴘᴏᴡᴇʀ Iɴᴄ. ʜᴀꜱ ʀᴇᴘʟɪᴄᴀᴛᴇᴅ ɪɴ Aᴜꜱᴛʀᴀʟɪᴀ ɪᴛꜱ ᴡᴏʀʟᴅ-wide success as a market leader in employment services. Retaining customers at a high level, as well as winning new ones, has produced exceptionally strong growth and enhanced the company's prestige. ⌒∞ Headquartered in Sydney since it was established in 1966, Manpower Services (Australasia) caters to every shape and size of

customer, from large international and multinational companies to small local businesses, as well as state and federal governments.

According to Chief Executive Officer Malcolm Jackman, the company wants to deliver the most innovative, consistent, and effective staffing solutions that enhance the business performance of clients. "Employers use us because we provide a very cost effective solution," he says. At the same time, Manpower strives to improve the lives of the people who provide those solutions, whether they work on a temporary or permanent basis.

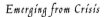

MANPOWER INC. PROVIDES AN ESSENTIAL EMPLOYMENT RESOURCE TO BUSINESSES IN AUSTRALIA. THROUGH THE COMPANY'S STATE-OF-THE-ART TRAINING AND PLACEMENT PROGRAMS, MODERN TECHNOLOGY HAS BEEN APPLIED TO MEET THE GOALS OF BOTH EMPLOYEES AND EMPLOYERS.

Emerging from Crisis

Manpower Inc. began its rise to prominence in 1948 amid an atmosphere of crisis. One night that April, Elmer Winter—an American lawyer living in Milwaukee—needed a typist to prepare an important brief. He called on a former secretary who had left her employment to start a family. Recognising that other compa-

nies had similar needs in times of emergency and during vacation and peak periods, Winter and his law partner, Aaron Scheinfeld, established Manpower's first service bureau, which became the foundation of modern employment agencies. Today, the company's 3,000 offices in more than 55 countries manage a work force of 2 million people.

In Australia, Manpower operated for most of its first three decades as a franchise until the parent company bought back the operation in late 1995. Since then, the number of offices in Australia and New Zealand has increased dramatically and continues to grow.

The overwhelming success of the entire Australasian operation has brought a new range of challenges, which have been met by Manpower's dedicated and loyal staff. "We have this unbelievable team of people with this huge passion about what they want to do, supported by the world's largest personnel services company," says Jackman. "So, we've got the local passion supported by a global vision from a global leader."

Technology and Employment

Modern technology has been applied in innovative ways to meet the goals of both employees and employers. For example, Manpower has created a virtual market through the development of a wide area network computer system. All of the company's service locations in Australia are linked into a single database so every office has access to the same information, and candidates for jobs can be sourced from anywhere in the country.

"Our computerised networking system allows us to provide 24-hour customer service, seven days a week, which is generally not common in our business," says Jackman. "We've essentially used our technology to make us considerably more intimate with our customers and more responsive to their needs." In addition, Manpower is equipped with a wide range of training opportunities, including the company's online global learning centre, which is best described as a campus on the Internet.

As the new millennium begins, Manpower anticipates significant growth, and its clear objective is to be the leader in the Australasian marketplace. Says Jackman, "The values of the organisation are that we want to be known as a champion team, as well as a team of champions."

THE COX GROUP IS ONE OF A SELECT FEW AUSTRALIAN architectural firms that have significantly contributed to the rise of Sydney as a world city. Along with the work of Harry Seidler and the singular intervention of Joern Utzon's Sydney Opera House, the transformation of much of Sydney's public realm has been the result of projects by the Cox Group. These include three major public buildings in

Darling Harbour; the city's major Bicentennial redevelopment; the Sydney Football Stadium; and Star City, the $780 million casino and theatre complex also in Darling Harbour.

Cox Group work is broadly represented in the new facilities for the Olympic Games, and these will largely portray the image of Sydney to the world in 2000.

Evolution

Philip Cox began private practice in 1964 with renowned Sydney architect Ian McKay. Together with several other small firms at the time, Cox and McKay developed an architecture that was to become identified as the Sydney School, which was acclaimed for its direct responsiveness to the Australian landscape and climate, using rugged, exposed structures and raw materials reminiscent of the Australian vernacular. The Sydney School, ironically, coincided with the work of a number of West Coast USA architects such as Joseph Eshcrick and Charles Moore, who were pursuing their own responses to similar landscape and climatic conditions.

Cox and McKay's first major commission—the C.B. Alexander Agricultural College at Tocal north of Sydney—epitomises the style of the Sydney School. Cox was later able to adapt the philosophy to many urban projects in central Sydney. His 1984 Yulara Tourist Resort, near Ayers Rock, fully explored the style's potential by using a passive energy design that was highly innovative for its time.

The fullest expression of Cox's structural ideals came with commissions for several major sports facilities in Canberra, Melbourne, and Sydney, as well as exhibition centres in Brisbane, Sydney, and Singapore for which the Cox Group is now renowned. Mostly undertaken with engineers Ove Arup & Partners, these buildings push the limits of structural technology and efficiency—characteristics that have become hallmarks of Cox Group design.

International Reach

The Cox Group's reputation for innovative design and powerful civic identity spread internationally in the 1990s. In addition to its offices in Sydney, Brisbane, Melbourne, Perth, and Canberra, the group opened branches in Singapore and Jakarta, participating in the rapid

PATRICK BINGHAM-HALL

PATRICK BINGHAM-HALL

development of South-East Asia with major master plan and design projects to its credit.

Major projects include the main stadium and aquatic centre for the 1998 Asian Games in Bangkok; office development in China and Indonesia; the 60,000-square-metre Singapore Expo Convention and Exhibition Centre; and the master plan for Bandar Nusajaya, a new city located on the Malaysian side of the second crossing being built between Singapore and Johor. In addition, the Cox Group created the master plan for Maritime Square, a redevelopment of 22 hectares of Singapore's docklands. Won by the firm in international competition following the world competition success for Singapore Expo, Maritime Square will further cement the Cox Group's position as leading global architects and planners.

The firm also was responsible for the Australian Pavilion at the Venice Biennale, one of the few contemporary buildings in that city. Additionally, the Cox Group won an international master planning competition for two new Kuwaiti cities in 1990.

Diversification and Specialisation
One of the major reasons for the Cox Group's escalation is its diversification into urban planning, urban design, and regional planning. Simultaneously, the group became a leading interior, health, and environmental designer, adding specialisation to diversity.

The Cox Group, nevertheless, maintained its earlier core ingredients, and these particularly resulted in the work for the Sydney Olympic Games. This body of work includes the Sydney International Aquatic Centre, the Sydney International Athletic Centre (with Peddle Thorp Architects), the relocated Royal

Agricultural Showground main arena/baseball stadium and pavilions (with Peddle Thorp and Conybeare Morison), and a new, 20,000 spectator, multiuse sports/entertainment centre, the Sydney SuperDome.

"Our clients now run the gamut from large public institutions and authorities to clients wanting designs for a holiday house, and we have consciously avoided being catalogued into any one sector of development," says Cox, founder and principal of the practice.

Recognition
The Cox Group is internationally recognised through such major awards as the Sir Robert Matthew Commonwealth Association of Architects Award for innovative contribution to design throughout the Commonwealth, and the International Olympic Committee (IOC) Award for Sports Architecture. Some 30 major awards from the Royal Australian Institute of Architects, as well as significant tourism, commercial, and engineering awards, are testimony to the Cox Group's consistently high standards of service. In 1988, a year after he was made an

Honorary Fellow of the American Institute of Architects, Cox received the Australian Federal Government's Order of Australia for services to architecture.

The Cox Group believes, however, that it is client recognition, whether a specific user or the public at large, that means the most. "There is architecture for architects," Cox says, "and architecture for people—the latter is for me the driving force."

Directions
The Cox Group, now with some 200 staff, will enter the new millennium with firm ideas on where the future lies. "Environmentally sustainable design will be the vital ingredient in any architecture to come, and there will be a lot more emphasis on collaborative design with specialists such as artists, industrial designers, and technology innovators," says Cox. "We will be striving in these directions and hopefully continuing to create meaningful and relevant architecture in response to the challenges of the new millennium."

PATRICK BINGHAM-HALL

COURTESY THE COX GROUP

Preformed Line Products (Australia) Pty Ltd

REFORMED LINE PRODUCTS (AUSTRALIA) PTY LTD (PLP) is a recognised leader in the development, manufacture, and marketing of products for overhead transmission and distribution powerlines, and optical-fibre and copper-cable systems, as well as in building data communication systems. PLP dominates specific niche markets in the industry, and its success has been driven by dedication to customer service.

NORMAN WINDELL SERVES AS MANAGING DIRECTOR OF PREFORMED LINE PRODUCTS (AUSTRALIA) PTY LTD (PLP).

PLP's customer service is supported by a pool of expertise developed and maintained by a long-standing team and a can-do attitude that influences all its activities.

PLP has been in Sydney since 1967, when it moved from Victoria into a newly constructed plant in the burgeoning western suburbs. In 1998, highlighting the steady success of PLP, the company moved into new headquarters and a plant complex at Glendenning.

Diverse Range of Products

Norman Windell, PLP Managing Director, explains that the extensive and diverse range of the company's products can most easily be described as the fittings that anchor expensive overhead cable infrastructure systems on transmission, distribution, optical fibre, and cable television lines. "The fittings that hold up the cables need to be very precisely engineered so as to hold the cable firmly, but at the same time prevent damage to the cable system," says Windell. "There are environmental issues to consider, such as adverse weather conditions, which could cause vibration, high loading, or clashing. Fittings need to protect the cable infrastructure from those conditions as best as possible."

PLP products that support and protect the expensive lines include insulator set fittings, vibration dampers, spacers and spacer/dampers for bundled conductors, cast-aluminum transmission line fittings, and insulator ties and stay fittings. Communications products include optical fibre cable splice cases and accessories, as well as cable fittings.

PLP has developed many new products for the industry in response to customer needs. The company first analyses customer requirements, then designs and engineers products to meet the needs of individual customers. PLP applies its in-house expertise to find solutions, bringing into account many scientific disciplines, ranging from mechanical to electrical engineering. "We rely on the parent company, and other PLP subsidiaries, to support us in some ways, but the bulk of the products that we manufacture have been engineered for the local market," says Windell.

The highest-quality materials are used in manufacturing production. The company is proud it has been ISO 9002 certified since 1992, ensuring its customers that its standards are the highest calibre. PLP also operates a NATA-accredited mechanical testing laboratory to test mechanical tension and metallic coating.

Engineering, production, sales, and management operations are undertaken from the company's new,

PLP'S MODERN, NEW OFFICE, FACTORY, AND LABORATORY COMPLEX IS LOCATED IN THE SYDNEY SUBURB OF GLENDENNING. THE COMPANY'S WEB SITE CAN BE FOUND AT HTTP://WWW.PREFORMED.COM.AU.

Teamwork is a hallmark of PLP's Sydney operation. Autonomous teams are established to solve specific problems that are presented by a client.

modern facilities, comprising 8,700 square metres. Of this, 6,100 square metres are dedicated to production facilities that include helical wire forming. Fifty of its more than 80 staff members are employed in the manufacturing sector of the company.

Proactive Success

PLP is a proactive company, with a policy of continuous activity in the marketplace. "We do go into the marketplace looking for new opportunities to unearth and new products to develop. We don't develop new products off our own back. We generally develop them in conjunction with customers to meet their needs," explains Windell.

Teamwork is a hallmark of PLP's Sydney operation. Autonomous teams are established to solve specific problems that are presented by a client. Research and development efforts are combined with the company's sophisticated high-tech software and equipment to support the increased productivity and quality of the work of PLP's staff. For example, sales staff use the latest technology to demonstrate to customers a three-dimensional model of a new product on a computer screen.

PLP divides its customers into four categories. A sales manager is in charge of each section, with responsibility for supporting customers by formulating solutions. In the energy and rail sector, customers include all the Australian electrical utilities. Customers in the contractors sector include ABB, Kilpatrick Green, and Transfield. Telstra and Optus Vision are among PLP's communications sector customers. The fourth sector is exports, where the company has enjoyed success on many of the major cable infrastructure projects in the Asia-Pacific region.

Expansion

PLP's parent company was originally established in Cleveland, Ohio, in 1947. PLP Australia became a wholly owned subsidiary in 1978.

PLP's Australian operation has regional responsibility for South-East Asia and the Pacific, and in June 1998, established an Asian regional office in Manila. In South-East Asia and New Zealand, the company works with local distributors who undertake the primary sales role. While the trend for Australian companies is to manufacture offshore, PLP has made a substantial investment in its new Sydney plant to maintain its production capacity onshore.

In early 1999, the company established a high-technology production area within the new Glendenning facility to manufacture a range of products for the data communications industry.

The employees of PLP have many years of experience in the industry, and have acquired a wealth of knowledge ranging from marketing to engineering to production expertise. Australian staff contribute and participate in the international operation's ongoing comprehensive training programs, which are developed as new products are introduced. It is company policy to support staff members undertaking continuing education by providing flexible working conditions and financial assistance to pay for their courses of study.

With a can-do attitude that places flexibility, customer service, and understanding of the customer's needs at the fore, PLP will continue to be a leader in its industry.

PLP's products are tested in the company's NATA accredited laboratory facility.

Walker Corporation Limited

Walker Corporation Limited is a leading national property developer, property manager, and major construction company that has been a significant force in reshaping the Australian built environment. The company is especially recognised for its high-quality residential development on the foreshores of Sydney Harbour, as well as areas overlooking it, which include the eastern suburbs, the southern and

northern shores of the harbour, tracts along the Parramatta River, and the lower north shore to Manly.

Walker has been instrumental in reshaping the traditional development and design approach that has been implemented in Sydney over the course of the city's history. Sydney was developed with an English mentality that basically addressed the need of constructing streets rather than the need to create houses that give their occupants the best possible views of their surroundings. Walker's philosophy is to turn this approach around and build residences that provide the best views, particularly those over Sydney Harbour. The company actively searches for sites that have the best outlooks and weather environments.

Challenges

As Walker has grown, the company has taken on more challenges. It has begun to develop sites that were once thought impossible to remediate and convert for adaptive uses. Applying its skills in many sciences, ranging from civil engineering to landscaping,

Walker has been able to give a new lease of life to large tracts of former industrial land that it has acquired in popular areas, such as those within the city near the water.

Walker was the only company to successfully design a package of redevelopment solutions for residential use of the wharf at Woolloomooloo— a major project that is rejuvenating a run-down but historic area of Sydney. The project's technical brief required the company to develop solutions for renovating the 100-year-old timber structure—which had been rotting away—so it would last for another 100 years. After two years of problem solving, Walker produced a solution, and the project is now nearing completion.

In a city that is famed for its real estate boom-and-bust cycles,

Walker has secured its stability through strategic diversification aimed at balancing short- and long-term activities in different building sectors. Walker's competitive edge in developing business environments can be seen in the broad array of structures it has created in retail, commercial, industrial, and residential developments.

Walker offers a full commercial relocation project service, promising to complete the relocation while the client continues to operate its business without interruption. The service includes all aspects of a relocation, including constructing new premises and improving the old premises' adaptive reuse. The success of Walker's relocation service is confirmed by the firm's many repeat clients.

The success and achievements of Walker Corporation Limited have resulted from the technical, architectural, and management skills that its personnel have applied in creating products that people want, such as this Balmain Cove village lifestyle (left).

Walker successfully designed redevelopment solutions for residential use of the wharf at Woolloomooloo. Pictured here are terraces next to the partially reconstructed finger wharf (right).

CLOCKWISE FROM TOP:
THE COMPANY IS ESPECIALLY RECOG-
NISED FOR ITS HIGH-QUALITY RESIDEN-
TIAL DEVELOPMENT ON THE FORESHORES
OF SYDNEY HARBOUR, AS WELL AS
AREAS OVERLOOKING IT. SHOWN HERE
IS A TYPICAL WALKER APARTMENT.

WALKER ACTIVELY SEARCHES FOR
SITES THAT HAVE THE BEST OUTLOOKS
AND WEATHER ENVIRONMENTS, SUCH
AS THESE TERRACE HOUSES AT BALMAIN
COVE.

WALKER DOES MOST OF ITS OWN
CONSTRUCTION WORK, APPLYING
SKILLS IN MANY SCIENCES, RANG-
ING FROM CIVIL ENGINEERING TO
LANDSCAPING.

History

Walker Corporation Limited began in an intere-housing contractor, with one machine and one truck. Lang Walker and his father, Alec, founded A & N Walker Pty Ltd in 1967. In the 1970s, the company was building roads and was involved in subdivision development. By the late 1970s, it had commenced developing residential properties.

In 1991, the Walker Group developed its first retail shopping centre, followed by its first multistage medium-density residential development in 1992. Known today as the Walker Corporation, the company was introduced on the Australian Stock Exchange in 1994. Lang Walker remains the managing director, and he is still the driving force behind the company, of which he owns 50 per cent. Today, Walker Corporation has revenues that exceed $500 million per annum, a staff of more than 300 people, and more than 1,000 subcontractors and contractors at any given time.

The company's success and achievements have resulted from the technical, architectural, and management skills that its personnel have applied in creating products that people want. By taking on challenging civil engineering projects, the company has attracted many talented people to its staff whose abilities, in turn, have enhanced the company's skills base. Walker has a team of people who have remained with the company through its international growth with the company.

Community

Community involvement for Walker means directly addressing issues that affect people in the areas where it does business. The company believes that its contributions to community welfare should be given as directly as possible to the people who need it. Typical of this approach was Walker's involvement with community activities in a major Sydney inner-city retail development project. After consultation with the local council, Walker set aside a large area for basketball courts. The company also made a grant to the council to employ a youth liaison officer to work in conjunction with the retail centre's management and to assist in programs that enhance the lifestyle of local youths.

In recognition of the excellence that it has achieved, Walker has won a wide range of industry awards over the years from organisations such as the Master Builders Association and the Housing Industry Association. By working in the sectors it knows best, Walker Corporation is certain to have many years of future success in creating built environments for Sydney's residents and businesses, which it will continue to serve well into the new millennium.

SUZANNE GRAE CORPORATION PTY LTD IS A SPECIALTY CHAIN of women's fashion stores for the budget- and fashion-conscious shopper. Since the first store opened in 1968, Suzanne Grae has provided customers—just as its motto says—with "good honest basics at good honest prices". The company's stores carry a variety of women's easy-care, easy-wear daily apparel, including casual, weekend, and work-wear separates.

A key feature of the apparel sold by Suzanne Grae is that it suits customers of any age, although the target market is women between the ages of 35 and 45. In addition, a selection of smart jewelry and accessories is available at Suzanne Grae stores across Australia.

A History of Growth

The Suzanne Grae headquarters is located in Silverwater, near the Homebush Bay area, future home of the 2000 Olympic Games and the demographic centre of Sydney. Suzanne Grae stores are located throughout the country, particularly in New South Wales. With a staff of more than 1,000 in 200 stores across mainland Australia, Suzanne Grae sells some 4 million garments each year.

The first Suzanne Grae store was opened in Wagga Wagga in 1968 by independent retailer John Hommann. By 1986, the chain had grown to 100 stores across Australia. In 1988, the family-owned Besen Corporation bought Suzanne Grae from Hommann. In addition to Suzanne Grae, Besen Corporation's portfolio includes the Sussan chain of stores, which is also a leader in the fashion apparel industry. With the combination of both labels, Besen has the largest independent holding of women's fashion stores in Australia.

Competitive Edge

Proud of the careful attention to detail that it gives to all the garments it sells, Suzanne Grae develops clothing designs in-house and in conjunction with suppliers, rather than buying ready-made lines. Suzanne Grae's commitment to customer satisfaction is paramount. Every garment line is developed to Suzanne Grae's exacting specifications.

The company's buying team conducts extensive research for its designs and works with suppliers to develop exclusive garments that will carry the Suzanne Grae house brand label. Company buyers travel around the world each season to stay abreast of changes in the fashion industry. Suzanne Grae's staff members are skilled in observing international trends and interpreting them to suit customers' tastes and preferences.

In order to provide convenient access for customers, the vast majority

IN ORDER TO PROVIDE CONVENIENT ACCESS FOR CUSTOMERS, THE VAST MAJORITY OF SUZANNE GRAE STORES ARE LOCATED WITHIN SHOPPING CENTRES, SUCH AS THIS ONE IN SYDNEY'S LIVERPOOL SHOPPING CENTRE.

◄ TONY YEATES MIDNIGHT

of Suzanne Grae stores are located within shopping centres. All of the stores possess an ambience that creates a warm and welcoming atmosphere and a user-friendly environment. Staff are always available to offer assistance if it is desired, and there is never pressure to buy.

Suzanne Grae's research has revealed that understanding and meeting the customer's needs is the pivotal ingredient in its success, and to continue to meet this goal, the company has devised a detailed training program to help the staff in stores improve critical customer service skills. Recruitment guidelines now emphasise that new staff must have an extremely strong customer focus.

As the company continues to grow, many more career path opportunities are being created for staff within the company. Suzanne Grae's success has been achieved with a shift away from the former task-oriented focus to the current strong focus on customers. It is a win-win situation for both the company and the employee.

Management is continuing to further decentralise many decision-making processes regarding day-to-day issues and distribution of resources to staff in the local stores. This move is being supported by improved use of information technology systems.

Loyalty Program

Suzanne Grae has built long-term relationships with regular customers by rewarding their loyalty. More

than half a million customers on the company's mailing list receive regular newsletters that include special offers and information about the latest merchandise.

Honesty and trust are core values that cement the relationship between Suzanne Grae and its customers. Prices are clearly marked and cannot be misread. Customers can be confident of Suzanne Grae's responsibility towards its customers. Under the company's refund policy, there are no questions asked, and the cost of the returned purchase is always refunded. Additionally, the customer is treated with the same courtesy when returning goods as when buying them.

The company is constantly refining its business practices to achieve

a higher level of excellence in performance. After some difficult years, Suzanne Grae has made significant gains through revised internal procedures and the enhancement of its profile in the marketplace. By providing customers with excellent service and by raising standards in the industry as a whole, Suzanne Grae will continue to be a leader in the fashion marketplace well into the new millennium.

▲ JOHN BARRETT

Sydney Convention & Visitors Bureau

THANKS TO THE SUCCESS OF THE SYDNEY CONVENTION & Visitors Bureau (SCVB), the capital of New South Wales has emerged as one of the world's leading travel destinations. Along the way, SCVB has turned this sector of the tourism industry into an economic boom for Sydney, bringing in billions of dollars annually. ❧ Established in 1969, the SCVB is the primary marketing organisation promoting

THE SYDNEY CONVENTION CENTER AT DARLING HARBOUR (LEFT)

CLARKE ISLAND IN SYDNEY HARBOUR IS A UNIQUE LOCATION FOR SPECIAL EVENTS (RIGHT).

Sydney as a gateway to Australia and a destination for meetings, incentive travel, conventions, and events (MICE) tourism. This lucrative marketing venture—to sell Sydney as Australia's premier city and a national gateway and MICE destination—was a joint effort with funding from the New South Wales Government and the tourism and travel industry. And while the focus of SCVB has remained unchanged, the group has grown considerably, from a mere two staffers to its current number of 25.

The bureau serves as a key point of contact, offering free advice and assistance to anyone interested in planning MICE activities in Sydney. SCVB represents 500 members from across the sector, who are providers of expertise in fields ranging from catering to convention coordinating.

"Sophisticated strategic and tactical sales and destination marketing activities, together with advisory services, are designed to deliver measurable results for the bureau's members and major stakeholders," says Jon Hutchison, managing director. SCVB is a nonprofit organisation funded by the state government of New South Wales, major sponsors, the City of Sydney, and SCVB's 500 members.

Success

As one of the largest bureaus in Australia, SCVB is a leader in the MICE sector. The organisation works closely with bureaus from other capital cities, exchanging promotional ideas and information. Through SCVB's work, Sydney has built a formidable reputation in the tourist industry. Readers of the respected *Condé Nast Traveler* magazine have voted Sydney as the World's Best City four years in a row, based on a number of criteria, including restaurants, amenities, and the friendliness of its citizens. Additionally, readers of *Business Traveller Asia-Pacific* magazine voted Sydney First in the World in a favourite city poll for two years running. Statistics from the International Congress and Convention Association identified Sydney as the world's Number One Convention City for 1997.

Expertise

When an organisation seeks the assistance of the bureau, a business development executive is appointed to work with the client to coordinate all aspects of a group's proposal, ensuring painstaking attention to the smallest details. The executive can also assist the clients with advice on securing government funding for international proposals, organising familiarisation and site inspections, and providing advice on incentive travel programs and special events.

Through its five departments, SCVB caters to the needs of members and promotes Sydney's strengths as a destination capital. Using SCVB research, the group's sales team bids for opportunities for Sydney to host national and international meetings, incentive travel programs, conventions, exhibitions, and special events. The marketing and communications department then produces publications that promote its members and Sydney to local and international contests, as well as the media. SCVB maintains a company Web site and produces newsletters, as well as the *Sydney Facilities Guide*.

The membership department services the needs of the bureau's 500 members through networking, education, and information sessions. This arm of SCVB secures the involvement of key Sydney businesses within the MICE industry. The databases compiled by the bureau's information resources division include a listing of industry members and statistics on Sydney's and Australia's MICE tourism sector. Corporate event organisers and convention and meeting planners can contact SCVB's members through the sales lead service, which

puts planners and organisers in touch with bureau members who can meet their needs.

An Economic Contributor

MICE revenue contributes significantly to the economy of Sydney. According to one study, international convention delegates spend nine times as much as the average international leisure tourist. During one period, SCVB won 24 conventions, accounting for 89,000 delegates staying a total of 145,000 days, and generating a more than $111 million boost to the local economy. Other bids have been won for future conventions through

to 2010. With the opportunity to promote Sydney in light of its hosting of the 2000 Olympic Games, the bureau highlighted the new and refurbished infrastructure dedicated to MICE events.

SCVB's representatives in North America and Europe form the cornerstone of its international direct sales efforts. Attending trade shows, roadshows, and key industry events, the bureau's representatives promote Sydney, distributing SCVB's publications to key contacts, generating media interest in Sydney, and ensuring that international media contacts have up-to-date information on members' products and services. Representatives gather market intelligence, undertake competitive analysis to identify potential clients, and develop bid opportunities.

SCVB's specialisation in promoting the MICE sector has led to exceptional results. Sydney has drawn some of the largest conferences in the world, and is set to continue attracting more international and domestic events as the city emerges on the world stage as a premier destination for business and tourism.

CLOCKWISE FROM TOP LEFT:
THE SYDNEY HARBOUR BRIDGE

THE SYDNEY OPERA HOUSE IS LOCATED ON ONE OF THE WORLD'S MOST RECOGNIZED LOCATIONS.

THE RESTAURANTS OF THE ROCKS ARE NESTLED BELOW THE SYDNEY HARBOUR BRIDGE.

AN AUSTRALIAN ABORIGINAL DANCE PERFORMANCE IS A MUST FOR ALL VISITORS TO SYDNEY.

SYDNEY HARBOUR IS THE PERFECT BACKDROP FOR NEW YEAR'S EVE CELEBRATIONS.

Young & Rubicam Inc

YOUNG & RUBICAM INC IS A WORLD LEADER IN MARKETING communications and brand building. Sydney is the headquarters for the Australia operations, one of the largest communications groups in the country, with companies specialising in all forms of brand communications. The firm's major clients include Citibank, Colgate-Palmolive, Mitsubishi Motors, Andersen Consulting, Coles Myer,

SYDNEY IS THE HEADQUARTERS FOR THE AUSTRALIA AND NEW ZEALAND OPERATIONS OF YOUNG & RUBICAM INC, ONE OF THE LARGEST COMMUNICATIONS GROUPS IN THE REGION. THE GROUP COMPRISES VARIOUS COMPANIES SKILLED IN ALL FORMS OF MARKETING COMMUNICATIONS. YOUNG & RUBICAM'S HEADQUARTERS ARE CLEARLY DENOTED AT THE NORTH SYDNEY ADDRESS. PICTURED IS CHAIRMAN AND CEO PETER STEIGRAD (LEFT).

Y&R PRODUCED A HIGHLY CREATIVE CAMPAIGN FOR RAY BAN (RIGHT).

National Dairies, Nintendo, Schweppes, and Ericsson.

Three of the leading Young & Rubicam companies in Sydney are Y&R Advertising, WCJ, and Burson-Marsteller. Together, these three offer clients a potent and creative mixture of brand communications in the mainstream advertising, direct, and loyalty management areas, as well as highly developed perception management capabilities.

Best Alone. Better Together.
While the three companies specialise in their specific areas and are con-

stantly challenged to be the best communications partners for their clients, they often partner with each other under a credo called Best Alone. Better Together.

The group's focus is on ensuring that each of its companies is the best at creating its own specialised communications. The group wants Y&R Advertising to be the best and most creative general advertising partner for clients. To do this, the focus is on creativity and on knowing more about the relationships between brands and consumers than any other agency. Y&R Advertising

can prove that it is the best in this area, but challenges are always there.

At WCJ, the company is continuing to develop the world's best resource at managing customers online and offline. This specialised area of direct communication involves data mining, database development and management, direct advertising, and multimedia and Internet communications to audiences that often are just single people at a time. As many commercial communications methods continue to fragment in order to reach customers, WCJ is the industry leader in embracing this change and leading the way forward in this exciting area.

At Burson-Marsteller, managing key stakeholder perceptions plays a vital role in the process of achieving corporate goals. The company is client focused and results oriented. The quality of its services is defined not just by the elements of process, creativity, and professionalism, but also by delivering the business results its clients seek to achieve.

White gets noticed.

For teeth so white they shine.

Leading-Edge Core Capabilities

Included in Burson-Marsteller's core capabilities is leading-edge expertise in financial communications, corporate reputation management, business-to-business marketing, public affairs, government relations, crisis communications, health care, consumer marketing, media relations, event marketing, organisational communications, and technology marketing.

Burson-Marsteller's key clients include Andersen Consulting, Unilever, Microsoft, Compaq, Roche, Eli Lilly, and Southcorp Ltd. Sydney's popular reputation as a tourist destination and launching pad for Australia's profit overseas often disguises the nature of business in the city.

Competition in business is always at the highest global standards. In Sydney and across Australia, there is intense rivalry among marketers for the attention of consumers. The country does not have a large population base, but the range of products and services available is indicative of First World countries having populations many times the size of Australia's.

This means that launching and growing a brand in this market is a huge challenge, and many fail. Burson-Marsteller shares its clients' business goals and brings to the table the best strategies, executions, and ideas to help grow brands. In some cases, where clients are already market leaders, the company's task is to constantly refresh a brand's relationship with its customers to fight off challenges from me-too products. There should never be a dull moment when managing a brand.

Shine, Australia, shine.

Burson-Marsteller makes some interesting points about managing communications. No one can isolate how and when target audiences make up their minds about products or issues. The company's business is about using communications to manage perceptions in order to change behaviours in a way that delivers desired business results to clients. In many cases, the quality of the communications is all that distinguishes a product or service

Tough guys.

Colgate Fluoriguard has strengthened more teeth and helped prevent more cavities than any other toothpaste in Australia. Only your dentist can give you a better fluoride treatment.

from its competition, so that quality has to be the best.

In addition to Burson-Marsteller, WCJ, and Y&R Advertising, the Young & Rubicam group of companies includes health care communications specialist company Sudler & Hennessey, Brand Dialogue multimedia communications, The Media Edge for media planning and buying, and Monica, a specialist multilingual communications company.

ONE OF YOUNG & RUBICAM'S MAJOR CLIENTS IS COLGATE-PALMOLIVE.

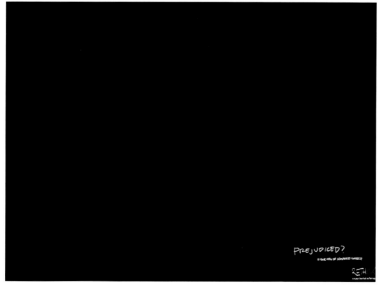

PREJUDICED?

NEWS LIMITED COMMISSIONED Y&R TO PRODUCE AN EVOCATIVE CAMPAIGN TO PROMOTE MORE CREATIVE USE OF NEWS PER ADVERTISING.

1971-1999

1971	Gemtec Pty Ltd
1971	Meinhardt (NSW) Pty Ltd
1972	Merrill Lynch (Australia) Pty Limited
1973	Medtronic Australasia Pty. Ltd.
1975	AM Corporation Ltd.
1978	KvB Institute of Technology
1981	AT&T Communications Services Australia Pty Limited
1982	Liebert Corporation Australia
1983	Corporate Relocations
1985	Citibank
1985	Michael Page International
1986	United Airlines
1989	FedEx
1991	Hotel Nikko Darling Harbour/Sydney
1992	Computer Associates International, Inc.
1992	Sydney Marriott Hotel
1994	Compuware Asia Pacific Pty Ltd
1995	New South Wales Department of State and Regional Development
1995	WorldxChange Communications
1996	AON Risk Services Australia Limited
1997	The Grace Hotel
1998	Towery Publishing, Inc.

G

EMTEC PTY LTD, WHICH BEGAN AS A ONE-MAN WHOLESALE gem merchant business, was established in 1971 by Maxwell Lane, a qualified gemmologist. Lane's vision for the new company was simple: To be the best, most highly thought of, and most reputable Australian company sourcing precious Australian gemstones for export. To accomplish this goal, the new company concentrated on selling quality

rather than quantity. "Gemtec specialised in the higher-quality end of the market, and that's paid off for us," says Lane.

In the beginning, the business involved sourcing Australian gemstones, processing them as required, exporting them overseas, and then importing overseas gemstones not found in Australia. But in the early 1980s, Gemtec stopped importing precious stones from overseas and began dealing solely in Australian gemstones, including Australian precious opals, Queensland boulder opals, black opals from Lightning Ridge, Argyle diamonds, and South Seas pearls from Broome.

Gemtec expanded to include mining, cutting and polishing, and sales through tax-free showrooms catering to tourists and international visitors. The company experienced major growth in the 1980s, and continues to grow steadily today. Gemtec now employs 150 people, and is recognised as one of Australia's largest opal companies specialising in tax-free and wholesale exports of

Australian gemstones. Gemtec operates tax-free stores in Melbourne and Perth, in addition to two stores in its home city of Sydney, the premier tourist entry point into Australia.

All of Gemtec's products are destined for the overseas markets, and the company has developed its export markets to include Southeast Asia, North America, and Europe. "We tend to market our wholesale products through the major whole-

sale jewellery fairs," says Lane. The company regularly exhibits at the major international fairs in Switzerland and Japan, and the prestigious New York gemstone jewellery fair.

Jewel Experts

Australia produces more than 90 per cent of the highest quality precious opals found anywhere in the world. Opals extracted in their rough form from Gemtec's mining bases, includ-

GEMTEC PTY LTD, WHICH BEGAN AS A ONE-MAN WHOLESALE GEM MERCHANT BUSINESS, WAS ESTABLISHED IN 1971 BY MAXWELL LANE, A QUALIFIED GEMMOLOGIST. GEMTEC NOW EMPLOYS 150 PEOPLE AND IS RECOGNISED AS ONE OF AUSTRALIA'S LARGEST OPAL COMPANIES SPECIALISING IN TAX-FREE AND WHOLESALE EXPORTS OF AUSTRALIAN GEMSTONES.

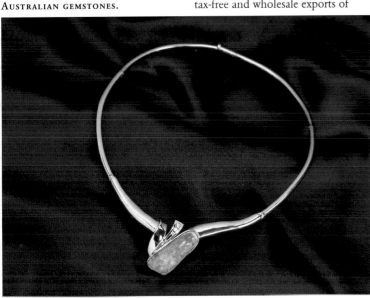

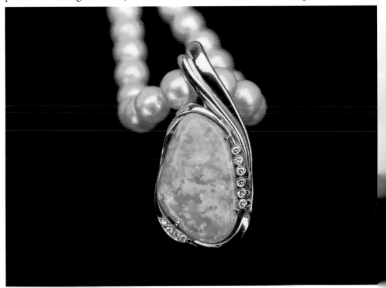

ing Coober Pedy in South Australia and Longreach in Queensland are flown to Lightning Ridge in New South Wales. There they are broken into manageable forms and flown to Gemtec's cutting factory in Sydney for processing.

The quality of the product from the processing depends entirely on the expertise of the gem cutter, a craft that has remained unchanged for many years. It is the care and attention to detail that extracts the best result from the raw material, and Gemtec is proud that its cutting and processing facility is one of the best in the world.

Lane is especially proud of his cutters, who are given training that Gemtec has developed over the years. "When we employ new cutters, we prefer to employ untrained people, so that we can train them ourselves in our own way of doing things, rather than try and retrain people who have learnt in a different way," Lane says.

Core Philosophy

Lane, Chairman and Managing Director of Gemtec, is very involved in all aspects of its business and operations. "It's very much a hands-on business for me. I'm still flying up every fortnight to the mining areas myself. And that's the side of the business that I enjoy the most, and always have."

Lane gives his team of executives, directors, and managers full autonomy within their responsibilities. This trust has been rewarded with loyalty from long-serving staff members who pass on the expertise they have gained through years of experience to new employees.

Vertical integration gives Gemtec a competitive edge. The company is able to apply the same rigorous standard of attention to detail in all aspects of mining, processing, and transforming the precious gemstones into jewellery for exporting.

A measure of Gemtec's success is that it has grown each year since its inception. Lane says there is no secret other than attention to detail, customer service, and pricing. Paramount in achieving success has been providing quality and value for money to customers, so that they become repeat customers. Gemtec is proud of its reputation of integrity, professionalism, and artistic skills. Says Lane, "The gemstone business is all about trust, and people trust us."

Bright Future

Gemtec has taken Mother Nature's gift to Australia, the unique opal, and used the craftsmanship of its skilled cutters to polish it into a resplendent jewel. Lane has made a successful business of providing opals at a reasonable cost. Gemtec's commitment to quality and service, coupled with the wealth of expertise and experience that it has acquired over the years, will continue to foster growth through the development of new export markets and tax free outlets within Australia.

"Many people have come and gone in this business, but we're here to stay. We are acknowledged throughout the world as being able to provide a recognised product at a good price," says Lane.

ALL OF GEMTEC'S PRODUCTS ARE DESTINED FOR THE OVERSEAS MARKETS, AND THE COMPANY HAS DEVELOPED ITS EXPORT MARKETS TO INCLUDE SOUTHEAST ASIA, NORTH AMERICA, AND EUROPE.

Meinhardt (NSW) Pty Ltd

MEINHARDT (NSW) PTY LTD HAS, IN ITS VERY SHORT HISTORY, become synonymous with engineering excellence. Founded by W.L. Meinhardt as a small structural engineering practice in 1955, this Australian enterprise has grown into an international multidisciplinary company of consulting engineers, project planners, and managers. Today, Meinhardt still leads the company as Executive Chairman, and under

his leadership, the firm expects continued international growth.

Meinhardt (NSW) Pty Ltd, a division of the Meinhardt Group, was established in Sydney in 1971 as the company's first step in its expansion throughout Australia. Whereas many companies grow through mergers and acquisitions, Meinhardt has grown through expansion. With reputation and success driving the company's growth, the 1970s saw the beginning of Meinhardt's international presence, opening its first overseas office in Singapore in 1972. Today, Meinhardt has a presence in 21 countries throughout Asia, the Middle East, and the Pacific, and employs more than 1,000 permanent staffers.

Multidisciplinary Approach
The company's team approach delivers innovative and creative solutions that are cost effective for clients. As a multidisciplinary engineering practice, Meinhardt offers services in every aspect of engineering and project planning and management. "We're a one-stop shop," says Denis Young, Managing Director

of Meinhardt (NSW) Pty Ltd. "We take an integrated and coordinated approach. We look at the various options and current technologies available, and incorporate them into our design in-house."

Although each division essentially looks after its local market, the Sydney office has worked on diverse projects in Vietnam and the Middle East. Clients include architects, builders, developers, project managers, and building owners. Among its noteworthy projects, the Sydney office was involved in the

acclaimed restoration of the prestigious Queen Victoria Building.

The company believes its staff is its most important asset in achieving its vision of providing quality engineering excellence. By working closely with clients and understanding their problems, Meinhardt staff members have built significant customer loyalty. Clients often return to the company not only for its vast array of services, but also for the highly trained people that provide those services.

Continued Success through Growth
"Our future goals include more expansion. In Australia, we're very well known as building engineers. We are expanding to include infrastructure in Australia, as well as in some of the developing countries," says Young.

Meinhardt wants to be the first choice among clients of all sizes, ranging from the smallest to the biggest. By providing a total engineering consulting service with cost-effective solutions, Meinhardt is set to grow in the new millennium, building its future on its internationally recognised expertise and global presence.

MEINHARDT (NSW) PTY LTD, A DIVISION OF THE MEINHARDT GROUP, IS AN INTERNATIONAL MULTIDISCIPLINARY COMPANY OF CONSULTING ENGINEERS, PROJECT PLANNERS, AND MANAGERS. THE FIRM'S PAST PROJECTS INCLUDE (CLOCKWISE FROM TOP) JOHN MADDISON TOWER, CAPITOL THEATRE, AND SUN ALLIANCE BUILDING.

WITH MORE THAN 100 YEARS OF EXPERIENCE, MERRILL LYNCH is a leading global financial management and advisory company with a presence in more than 45 countries across six continents and approximately 60,000 employees worldwide. Located in the hub of Australian commercial life, the Merrill Lynch Sydney office houses half of the Australasian division's staff of 808 and more than 50 financial consultants.

Merrill Lynch has been operating in Sydney since 1972. The company is Australia's second-largest stockbroker and has, through Merrill Lynch Mercury Asset Management, an asset management business of more than $5 billion in funds under management.

Long History

Since its beginning, Merrill Lynch, founded by Charles E. Merrill, has operated on the belief that opportunities in the markets should be accessible to everyone. It was Merrill's lifework to bring Wall Street to Main Street. Now, with total client assets of more than US$1.4 trillion, Merrill Lynch is the leader in planning-based financial advice and management for individuals and small businesses.

As an investment bank, it has been the top global underwriter of debt and equity securities for eight years running, and a leading strategic adviser to corporations, governments, institutions, and individuals worldwide. Through Merrill Lynch Asset Management and Merrill Lynch Mercury Asset Management, the company is one of the world's largest managers of financial assets.

Another focus of Merrill Lynch that originated with its founder is put-

ting the interest of the customer first. Today, this philosophy is expressed in five principles that define the way Merrill Lynch does business: Client Focus, Respect for the Individual, Teamwork, Responsible Citizenship, and Integrity. "Our plan in Autralasia is to be the leading provider of financial services by utilising our five guiding principles. They're on the doors when you come in and on people's desks," says David McWilliams, Managing Director for Merrill Lynch Private Client.

Defining Financial Goals

Merrill Lynch's financial consultants stress planning that considers a broad range of financial needs. The firm's consultants help clients define their financial goals, determine the amount of time they have to reach those goals, and establish their performance expectations.

A broad spectrum of services at Merrill Lynch is designed to tailor comprehensive strategies for managing clients' total portfolios. Merrill Lynch continues to enhance and develop products to accommodate client needs. In 1977, the first Cash Management Account was introduced, and has proved to be a powerful,

personal asset management tool for investing, saving, borrowing, and spending. Personal chequebooks and electronic funds transfers augment the value of these accounts. During the 1990s, acquisitions—which included Centaurus, a specialist corporate advice concern, and McIntosh Securities, a leading provider of financial services—led to an expansion of Merrill Lynch's services in Australia.

Merrill Lynch also provides a site on the World Wide Web that gives clients electronic access to information about the firm's products and services, specialised research, and asset and liability management, among other areas. The international Web site also provides a forum in which prospective and existing clients can contact the firm from anywhere in the world.

Whether assisting with mergers for large corporations or consulting with a young couple just beginning a financial portfolio, Merrill Lynch leads the way in providing trusted advice based on financial expertise, global perspective, and long-term view. The principles of client commitment that originated with Charles Merrill himself are effectively guiding the firm towards a successful future.

CLOCKWISE FROM TOP: MERRILL LYNCH (AUSTRALIA) PTY LIMITED PRINCIPALS INCLUDE DAVID MCWILLIAMS, MANAGING DIRECTOR, MERRILL LYNCH PRIVATE CLIENT; JOHN MAGOWAN, CO-CEO; DAVID SWAIN, CHIEF ADMINISTRATIVE OFFICER; AND STEVE DUCHESNE, MANAGING DIRECTOR, HEAD OF DEBT MARKETS.

THE FIRM'S CONSULTANTS HELP CLIENTS DEFINE THEIR FINANCIAL GOALS, DETERMINE THE AMOUNT OF TIME THEY HAVE TO REACH THOSE GOALS, AND ESTABLISH THEIR PERFORMANCE EXPECTATIONS.

MERRILL LYNCH'S FINANCIAL CONSULTANTS STRESS PLANNING THAT CONSIDERS A BROAD RANGE OF FINANCIAL NEEDS. WHEN THEY ARE NOT HARD AT WORK ON CLIENT PORTFOLIOS, MANY PARTICIPATE ON THE FIRM'S YACHT TEAM.

Medtronic Australasia Pty. Ltd.

When US-based Medtronic opened its Australasian headquarters in Sydney in 1973, the world's leader in implantable and interventional therapies was determined to achieve a prominent position in the medical technology marketplace. Promoting and distributing the products of its parent company, Medtronic Australasia Pty. Ltd. is today at the forefront of several market sectors, including pacemakers, implantable

CLOCKWISE FROM TOP:
DR. PETER BARRETT AND MEDTRONIC'S NICOLE GADDI ANALYSE DATA FROM A MEDTRONIC PACEMAKER.

DR. DAVID PLATTS GUIDES A MEDTRONIC VASCULAR DEVICE DURING SURGERY.

PROFESSOR MICHAEL COUSINS IMPLANTS A MEDTRONIC DRUG PUMP PAIN MANAGEMENT UNIT INTO A PATIENT.

defibrillators, heart valves, and spinal cord stimulation equipment used for the treatment of lower back pain. It has also gained a considerable market share in other product areas. "We try and enhance the wellbeing of mankind by the application of biomedical engineering to provide the best possible products we can," says Warren Ryan, general manager of Medtronic Australasia since 1988.

In Sydney and across the world, Medtronic's intention is to forge a partnership with the medical community so that, together, they can alleviate pain, restore health, and extend life. In the process, the company strives to make a fair profit while always acting as an ethical corporate citizen. "It's important to state that we are here to make a fair profit, because without that, we would not be able to reinvest in research and development, and we wouldn't be able to support the medical community to the level that we do," Ryan says.

Focused on Training and Education

In addition to serving as Medtronic's Australasian headquarters, Sydney is a regional training and educational hub for the company. The well-equipped education facility, located within the Gladesville office, contains a sophisticated range of audiovisual equipment used for in-house training sessions for medical staff, as well as for Medtronic's own field sales force.

Under an innovative program begun in 1992, the company's sales staff has been exhaustively trained to understand medical problems and procedures. In fact, five Medtronic staff members have passed examinations set by NASPE (North American Society for Pacing and Electrophysiology), which specialises in anatomy, physiology of the heart, the conductivity system, and pacing. This level of expertise—unparalleled in the industry—creates an atmosphere of respect that ensures Medtronic's sales staff an easy entry into the region's health and medical institutions.

Building a Loyal Employee Base

Many members of Medtronic's Australasian management team have been with the company for more than a decade, proving that loyalty is a hallmark of the Sydney operation. Staff retention has been further improved in recent years, thanks to a major restructuring in the early 1990s that included the creation of national product divisions focused on marketing and selling the company's specialised technology. These enhancements—combined with a generous incentive program for all staff, not just the sales force—have proved to be yet another catalyst for growth and prosperity.

In recognition of its overall success, the Australasian division has won Medtronic's Global Cup, an award designed to encourage

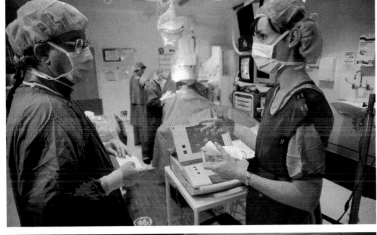

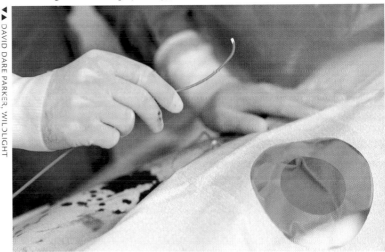

DAVID DARE PARKER, WILDLIGHT

DAVID DARE PARKER, WILDLIGHT

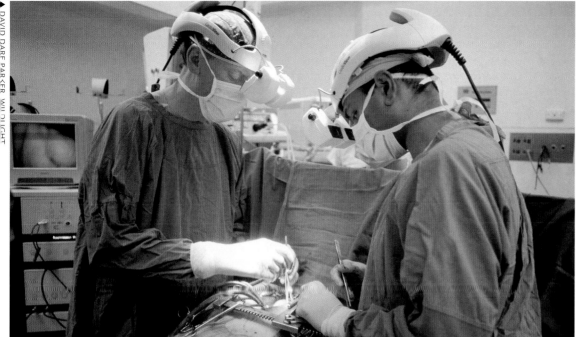

and salute performance within the company's geographic regions. Additionally, Ryan was honoured with the Wallin Leadership Award in 1996 for growing the Australasian operation 62 per cent over the previous year.

Serving Patients since 1949

Medtronic's global reach has its roots in a tiny American company founded in 1949. That year, Earl E. Bakken and his brother-in-law, Palmer J. Hermundslie, established a medical equipment repair business in a 600-square-foot garage in Minneapolis. From the beginning, they shared a vision "of contributing to the human welfare by the application of biomedical engineering to alleviate pain, restore health, and extend life."

The international operation, which remains headquartered in Minneapolis, has grown to encompass more than 20,000 staff in 120 countries, with an annual turnover of nearly US$4 billion. But that kind of success hasn't come without hard work and an ongoing commitment to innovation. Always at the forefront in the development of medical devices, Medtronic manufactured the first external battery-operated pacemaker in 1957.

In 1985, the company's Australasian operation was the first in Medtronic to release a rate-responsive, single-chamber pacemaker. Launched in the United States in 1986, the device senses the activity of the patient and adjusts the heart rate accordingly. Before that time, implanted pacemakers

could only achieve a programmable—but fixed—heart rate. Another first for Medtronic in the Southern Hemisphere was the introduction of deep brain stimulation, a pioneering procedure for treatment of the symptoms of Parkinson's disease, at Sydney's world-renowned St. Vincent's Hospital.

Opportunities Ahead

As it looks to the future, Medtronic will continue to market its own innovative products, as well as complementary technologies pioneered by other industry leaders. This approach allows Medtronic to lend its global reputation to other companies' technologies and products, while positioning itself to further grow revenues.

Another primary platform for growth will be Medtronic's commitment to identifying unmet medical needs, and developing the technology and products necessary to address them. The company's current focus

in its Neurological Division includes the treatment of Parkinson's disease and urinary incontinence, two challenging medical problems that predominantly affect the world's aging population. Further advances in the area of minimally invasive cardiac surgery will shape the future efforts on the company's Cardiac Surgery Division.

The Cardiac Rhythm Management Business continues to lead the cardiology and electrophysiology market with advances in ways to treat arrhythmias and other ailments of the heart. The Vascular Business is currently involved in expanding into providing products to treat vascular disease in other parts of the body.

Seeking advancements in these areas is one of many ways in which Medtronic lives up to its heritage of enhancing patients' lives and contributing to human welfare.

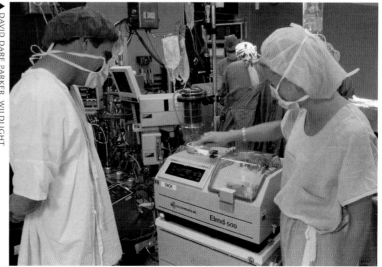

AM Corporation Ltd.

In 1975, David Smith founded AM Corporation Ltd. to give individual Australians access to Financial services of the same quality and value that he wanted for himself and his family. Today—with more than 100,000 clients and $2 billion in assets under management—the Sydney-headquartered AM Corporation has offices in every state, and is one of Australia's largest independent superannuation and

investment services providers. A 100 per cent-Australian-owned unlisted company, AM Corporation offers services that include public superannuation funds for individuals and employers; private superannuation fund (DIY, or do-it-yourself) establishment, administration, and consulting; life insurance; annuity contracts; and residential and commercial mortgages, among other areas.

"Our objective is to provide individual Australians with better value available in the wholesale markets, which is normally accessible only to corporations and large investors. This includes, for example, consistent, above average investment performance with the successful Managed Investment Managers [MIM] process," says Smith, who also serves as AM Corporation's chairman.

AM Corporation not only provides investors with great investment opportunities, but also supports those in need in the community with many donations and sponsorships given to community and charitable organisations. Each year, more than

5 per cent of the firm's profit is dedicated in this way to the people of Australia. Helping individual Australians and their families is at the core of the company's corporate belief.

Unparalleled Expertise

AM Corporation's expertise is widely recognised within the industry. The company's senior managers—the majority of whom have at least 15 years' experience in the financial services industry—are often asked to speak at financial industry seminars and conferences. Executive directors often prepare material for courses conducted by the Association of Superannuation Funds of Australia and the Financial Planning Association of Australia.

According to Smith, "Superannuation and investments are complex, and investors need advice from people who work for them, not advisers who work for the institution"; thus AM Corporation only offers its services through independent financial advisers and accountants. "We do not have our own sales force promoting AM products to members of the public," Smith says. "So you can be assured that the advice you get about AM from your financial adviser is always independent."

CLOCKWISE FROM TOP LEFT: IN 1975, DAVID SMITH FOUNDED AM CORPORATION LTD. TO GIVE INDIVIDUAL AUSTRALIANS ACCESS TO FINANCIAL SERVICES OF THE SAME QUALITY AND VALUE THAT HE WANTED FOR HIMSELF AND HIS FAMILY.

THE SYDNEY-HEADQUARTERED AM CORPORATION HAS OFFICES IN EVERY STATE, AND IS ONE OF AUSTRALIA'S LARGEST INDEPENDENT SUPERANNUATION AND INVESTMENT SERVICES PROVIDERS.

"TODAY, AM CONTINUES TO PROVIDE AUSTRALIANS WITH INNOVATIVE, HIGH-VALUE, AND COST-EFFECTIVE FINANCIAL SERVICES," SAYS SMITH.

Among the innovations pioneered by AM Corporation was the MIM style of investment, which the firm began in 1986. The principle that underlies MIM is that a team of several successful investment managers will produce better results than a single manager over a reasonable length of time. Moreover, the result will be produced more consistently and with lower volatility. Michael Devlin, AM Corporation's deputy chairman and chairman of the firm's investment committee, says, "Research confirms again and again that one manager cannot consistently maintain substantially, or even moderately, above average performance." Devlin adds, "The important skill in managing investment managers is selecting the right ones in the right category at the right time."

To provide clients with greater access to information about their accounts, AM implemented a 24-hour, high-tech telephone response system and a secure connection with the AM Internet Web site. Clients can order statements and obtain pertinent information regarding the performance of their investments.

Industry Innovations

Other innovations developed by AM Corporation have also become established trends in the industry. Over the years, AM's products and services have become diversified and have been developed to meet the needs of people in changing times. In 1997, AM Corporation established the first private pension fund that was specifically designed for Australian small business. In 1981, the company introduced the first

combined pension and lump sum fund in Australia. AM then established in 1985 the first superannuation fund to be approved by the Occupational Superannuation Commission—which became the Insurance and Superannuation Commission (now the Australian Prudential Regulation Authority)—and in 1986, the fund was the first to be ratified by the Australian Conciliation and Arbitration Commission. That same year also saw the establishment of LifeTrack, the nation's first public offering of a superannuation fund that accesses fund managers through AM Corporation's MIM process. LifeTrack achieved $100 million in assets, and by 1993, this figure had reached the $600 million mark.

"Today, with more than $2.7 billion of funds under management, AM continues to provide Australians with innovative, high-value, and cost-effective financial services," says Smith. "We aim to exceed client expectations by not only capturing financial market opportunities, but also continually providing opportunities through creative new services to help our clients achieve their financial goals."

THE KvB INSTITUTE OF TECHNOLOGY HAS GROWN DRAMATI-cally in the two short decades since its founding by Karl-Horst von Busse. The school's reputation for excellence in teaching the art and technology of visual design and communication has allowed it to grow from its original enrollment of 25 students into Australia's largest private design college, attracting students from all over Australia and overseas.

The aim of the KvB Institute is to give its students high-quality, hands-on training for a variety of creative careers in visual communication by remaining abreast of industry trends, using the latest industry-standard computer hardware and software, and attracting the best-quality teachers.

Although graphic design remains the core discipline at KvB, the school's academic courses have been developed over the last two decades to reflect the changing and increasing demands of students and the design professions. Today, the college offers courses ranging from fashion and photography to multimedia.

Von Busse arrived in Australia in 1960 from Germany, where he was born and educated. In 1972, von Busse established his own graphic design studio, KvB Visual Concepts, before founding the institute in 1978. As a member of the Design Institute of Australia, he is regularly invited to address both professional and academic groups in the field of design.

The vision and energy of von Busse continues to nurture the college's growth and success. He remains involved in the operation of the college, meeting regularly with students and teaching staff. His high standards, inspired by the desire to strive for perfection, influence the academic tone, the college's courses, and even its physical environment.

Accreditation

In a considerable accomplishment, the college was the first and remains one of the few non-university, private education providers in Australia

bestowed with the authority to grant degrees. It awards the bachelor of arts degree in visual communication, and is also accredited to award a range of diplomas and certificates.

Also attached to the college is the KvB Institute of Languages, which offers students from anywhere in the world the opportunity to learn English. Accredited by the National ELICOS (English Language Intensive Courses for Overseas Students) Accreditation Scheme, its courses are offered at four levels to meet the needs of students as they learn about their professions and chosen areas of general interest. Students can take specialised courses to prepare them for international language tests, such as University of Cambridge English Examinations.

Success

The KvB Institute of Technology prides itself on successfully preparing graduates to enter the competitive world of design with the means to be creative and productive. Von Busse founded the college because he wanted to train professionals who would be productive within a short period of time.

"He was looking to establish a more hands-on type of training. He wanted people to produce things, rather than talk about producing things," says Professor Tony Shannon, AM, PhD, the college's provost.

In carefully developed courses, theory and practice of visual communications are entwined into one fully rounded learning experience. Students are expected to produce work that is as good as that produced by working professionals.

Periods of internship with leading practitioners are integral components of the courses. The internships lead to offers of employment for many students, who also begin to build

networks from the contacts that they make.

Prime Location

The KvB Institute of Technology is located in the heart of Sydney's advertising, design, and computer industries in North Sydney. The prime location means the college can draw on the best people in the industry and professions for its teaching staff. In fact, the majority of the college's teaching staff are freelancers with their own practices.

"It's a good situation, because most teachers are bursting with enthusiasm. They share what they're doing with students. I was initially sceptical and thought we'd need more full-time staff. We've got the balance right at the moment, with about 20 full-time and about 70 part-time staff," Shannon says.

KvB's two main campuses, which are within a 10-minute walk of each other, each house television and photography equipment, studios, colour and black-and-white dark-rooms, and a teaching darkroom. The main campus is located in the KvB building in Mount Street, North Sydney. It was designed by the highly acclaimed architect Alex Popov, renowned for his work on the Sydney Olympic Games site.

The strength and creativity of the college are symbolised by the steel sculpture at the entrance of the college. It is a massive pencil and pad that, although anchored to the ground, sweeps the eye upwards to the facade of the KvB building. Inside, every-thing is designed to inspire students' creativity. The sleek, contemporary interiors house spacious, naturally lit classrooms overlooking the cityscape. Access to the latest tech-nology and equipment is available for each student, ranging from high-powered Macintosh computers to the best sewing machines. Each floor is thematically designed with a teacher's office at the centre.

As the college's reputation for excellence has spread internation-ally, the number of students and the number of different countries from which they come have increased steadily. The growing international student intake, together with its acknowledged quality of education, ensures that the KvB Institute of Technology will remain Australia's leader in teaching future generations of top design practitioners.

STUDENTS AT KVB INSTITUTE OF TECHNOLOGY UTILISE THE CONTROL ROOM DURING A TELEVISION PRODUCTION.

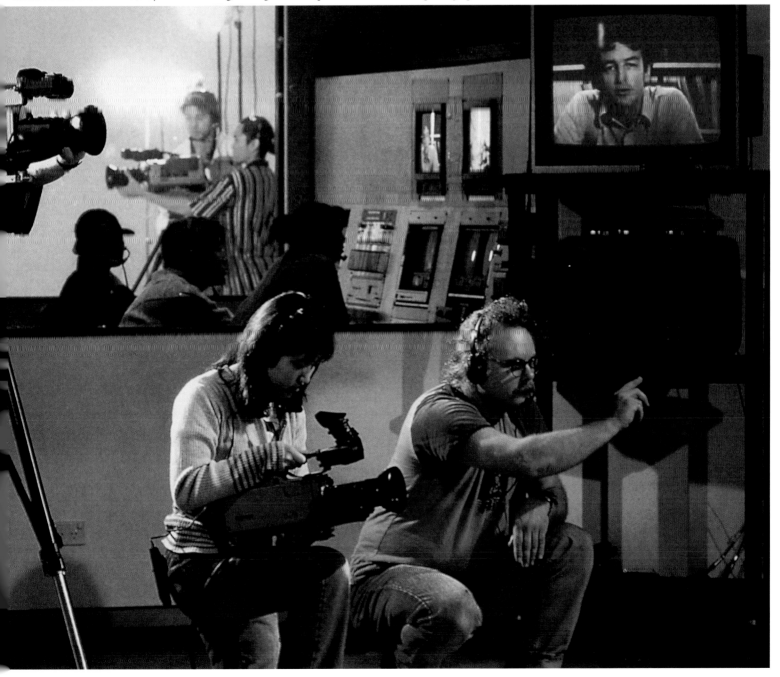

AT&T, THE WORLD'S PREMIER VOICE AND DATA COMMUNICA-tions company, opened its Sydney office in 1981. AT&T Communications Services Australia Pty Limited is the Australasian headquarters of the globally integrated AT&T Corporation. ✢ US-based AT&T Corporation has a long history, tracing its origins back to Alexander Graham Bell, who invented the telephone in 1876. The American

CLOCKWISE FROM TOP LEFT: THROUGH AT&T COMMUNICATIONS SERVICES AUSTRALIA PTY LIMITED, AUSTRALIAN CUSTOMERS HAVE ACCESS TO A WIDE RANGE OF HIGH-TECH COMMUNICATION AND INFORMATION SERVICES.

WITH MORE THAN 110,000 EMPLOYEES, AT&T CORPORATION MANAGES THE WORLD'S LARGEST AND MOST SOPHISTICATED COMMUNICATIONS NETWORK.

AT&T OFFERS A NUMBER OF VALUABLE SERVICES FOR LOCAL AND INTERNATIONAL BUSINESS AND CONSUMER CUSTOMERS.

Telephone and Telegraph Company—the forerunner of AT&T—was incorporated in New York City in 1885 as a division of American Bell Telephone Company. Its purpose was to manage and expand American Bell's long-distance business, as well as that of its licensees. Today, AT&T Corporation is the largest telecommunications company in the United States, and a worldwide leader in communications services.

Services

With more than 140,000 employees, AT&T Corporation manages the world's largest and most sophisticated communications network. Although AT&T's core business is long-distance services, the company is a leading provider of a wide range of voice, cable, video, Internet, and data communications. Some of the company's primary business units include AT&T WorldNet® services, AT&T Wireless Services, and AT&T Solutions consulting services. In addition, one of the company's major initiatives is the continued growth of local telephone service in the United States.

Australian Connection

Australian customers have access to a wide range of high-tech communication and information services, offering a number of valuable services for local and international business and consumer customers. Services include bilateral and multilateral voice and data services and systems, outsourcing for multinational companies and Australian businesses, and AT&T calling card products for the traveller market. In addition, AT&T's electronic commerce, Web hosting, Web site development and consulting, and electronic data interchange services deliver effective solutions to business clients.

Andrea Galloway, CEO and managing director of AT&T Communications Services Australia Pty Limited, says, "Our Australian base of customers includes Tradegate and the Australian Customs Service, as well as their trading partners, which include major transportation companies, freight forwarders, and customs brokers. Through this community network, we provide the infrastructure and solutions necessary to facilitate the transportation of goods in and out of Australia quickly and efficiently, in accordance with the requirements of the Australian Customs Service."

Australian Milestones

In 1880, Western Electric—a company that later became a longstanding manufacturing subsidiary of AT&T—sold its first telephone in Australia. In 1887, just two years after its founding, the American Telephone and Telegraph Company (AT&T) assisted Australia in the installation of its first telecommunications switching device. In 1934, AT&T won its first service agreement in Australia.

Forging ahead at the end of the 20th century, AT&T established the region's first Internet backbone network in 1995, which offers high-speed connections between Australia, Hong Kong, Japan, Korea, and the United States. InterCommerce, developed in Australia, was launched in 1997. It offers both multinational companies and small businesses effortless and affordable electronic document transfer.

Success

AT&T has grown into one of the world's leading telecommunications companies by aiming to enrich customers' personal lives and to make businesses more successful by providing innovative communications services. An annual revenue exceeding US$52 billion and a customer base of more than 80 million clients attests to AT&T's success in the world and in Australia.

GLOBAL FINANCIAL SERVICES GIANT CITIBANK OPENED FOR BUSINESS as a trading bank in Australia in 1985. With Australasian headquarters in Sydney, Citibank has aggressively pursued its vision to be "the preferred international bank in Australia and New Zealand, providing insight and global expertise—the best global bank locally and the best local bank globally." ❧ Since entering the market,

Citibank has been winning accolades from its half-million consumer and corporate customers, and, most significantly, from fellow bankers. Euromoney Publications, the prestigious international financial publisher, cited the organisation as the best foreign bank in Australia for four consecutive years. Citibank is also proud that its peers in the financial services industry have voted it the best foreign bank in Australia, an award organised by *Australian Banking and Finance* magazine.

"We know the local economy, markets, and industry conditions. What we can offer that most of our competitors can't is knowledge based on our global presence," explains Bill Ferguson, managing director. "We are able to provide our customers, especially our corporate customers, on-the-ground expertise just about anywhere in the world that they or their customers may be doing business."

An Emphasis on Corporate Banking

Founded in the United States in 1812, New York-based Citibank has established more than 3,400 offices in 100 countries worldwide to meet the diverse needs of its commercial and private customers. Today, across Australia and New Zealand, the company's services are successfully delivered by a staff of 1,600—nearly 500 of whom are part of Citibank's corporate banking division. In all their endeavours, these employees remain focused on the company's pioneering commitment to delivering personalised service that maximises benefit and profit potential for the customer. To that end, a relationship manager works with a team of Citibank experts to understand the

customer's business. Together, they think strategically and laterally about what financial arrangements will best support each customer's needs.

Corporate customers across Australia and New Zealand have benefited from Citibank's global expertise in areas such as project finance, loan syndications, trade, custody, and financial markets products. "We've been the global leader in the area of foreign exchange worldwide for the last 20 years," says Ferguson. Citibank has also been acclaimed as the leading foreign exchange bank for 20 consecutive years by Euromoney.

An Innovative Spirit

Always at the forefront in anticipating and meeting the needs of corporate customers, Citibank most recently launched Integrated Process Solutions (IPS). This new business initiative, a first in the Australian marketplace, offers corporate customers a cost-effective means of outsourcing a variety of financial administration functions.

In addition, both consumer and corporate customers benefit from Citibank's dedication to developing innovative, high-tech facilities and products. The company's gold and electronic banking products, in fact, are acknowledged as the top in their class.

But despite an impressive history of innovation and global expansion, Citibank is not resting on its laurels. In October 1998, the company merged with Travelers Group, bringing together two organisations committed to serving consumers, corporations, institutions, and governments through an array of global sales and service channels. The merged company,

known as Citigroup, will focus on traditional banking, consumer finance, credit cards, investment banking, securities brokerage and asset management, and property casualty and life insurance. This formidable combination makes Citigroup one of the largest financial services organisations in the world, and promises to enrich the selection of products available to meet the ever-changing needs of customers in Australia, New Zealand, and beyond.

WITH AUSTRALASIAN HEADQUARTERS IN SYDNEY, CITIBANK HAS AGGRESSIVELY PURSUED ITS VISION TO BE "THE PREFERRED INTERNATIONAL BANK IN AUSTRALIA AND NEW ZEALAND, PROVIDING INSIGHT AND GLOBAL EXPERTISE—THE BEST GLOBAL BANK LOCALLY AND THE BEST LOCAL BANK GLOBALLY."

In 1964, an American named Ralph Liebert assembled in his home garage in Columbus, Ohio, a prototype that would revolutionise how companies housed their sophisticated computer systems. He saw the potential for expanding his already successful airconditioning company by developing the niche market for controlled environments in the emerging mainframe computer industry. ❧ Liebert understood the

LIEBERT CORPORATION AUSTRALIA IS A TOTAL SOLUTIONS PROVIDER. WITH A DIVERSE PRODUCT RANGE AND VERY HIGHLY SKILLED EMPLOYEES, LIEBERT AUSTRALIA OFFERS INTEGRATED SOLUTIONS TO CLIENTS' PROBLEMS.

complexities involved in creating the exact environment that would protect a computer's sensitive electronics. He recognised the need to provide a computer room with adequate airflow to accommodate the high levels of heat that computers generate. The level of humidity was also a consideration, requiring different specifications to that of established airconditioning units. Liebert's precisely designed airconditioning systems for computer rooms addressed all these considerations in a single unit, creating an environment of constant air temperature and humidity levels. The prototype was satisfactorily tested by IBM in 1965, and the system was soon exhibited at an international industry show, where it received acclaim and many orders.

Controlling Power Systems

With the airconditioning problems solved, computers were still susceptible to an inconsistent power supply, especially where large computers operated over long periods. Conditioned Power Corporation was established by Liebert Corporation in 1978 to address these concerns, which were particularly problematic in the data processing industry. In 1981, Liebert became a publicly traded company, and in 1983, Liebert acquired California-based Programmed Power Division, thus bringing into its arsenal expertise in uninterruptible power supply (UPS) systems, which provide a continuous supply of power that is free of sudden surges and outages.

Today, the company generally serves data centres and telecommunications companies that need highly specialised cooling systems and continuous power. With the growth of the LAN and WAN network systems, Liebert has also successfully become a major supplier of smaller UPS products and enclosure systems for the computer networking industry. Liebert's operations have grown steadily in this field by building on the company's expertise base in order to develop new and improved products, and to achieve better solutions to power problems.

In March 1987, Liebert was acquired by the Emerson Electric Company, a St. Louis-based corporation engaged principally in the manufacture and sales of electrical/electronic products and systems. Emerson is one of the most admired companies in the United States, with annual revenue of some US$12 billion in 1997,

Australia

In 1982, Liebert Corporation established its Australian operations, which are headquartered in Sydney. The company is represented throughout the country with offices in the Australian Capital Territory, Victoria, Queensland, and Western Australia. In addition, Liebert Corporation Australia has achieved success with its export of airconditioning products to China and to South-East Asia through various distribution channels.

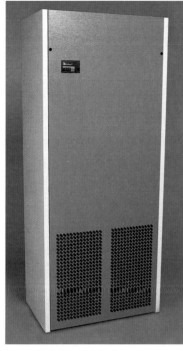

The present Liebert Australian operation comprises a combination of both Liebert and Atlas Air Australia personnel. This follows the acquisition of Atlas Air Australia by Liebert in October 1993. Atlas Air was a locally owned manufacturer and distributor of quality computer room airconditioning products. Liebert chose to continue manufacturing the Atlas Air Australian product after the acquisition. Because the Atlas name is so highly regarded in the Australian airconditioning field, Liebert continues to use the Atlas name on its line of precision airconditioners. This acquisition brought together talented and dedicated people from both companies whose combined efforts transformed two previously competitive companies into a jointly profitable member of Liebert's worldwide operations. Since both companies had plants in Regents Park, in Sydney's western suburbs, the two were integrated into Liebert's facility.

Liebert's research and development division is one of the strongest in the Australian airconditioning field. The company's longstanding and highly respected engineers operate from a sophisticated laboratory with high-tech equipment that can thoroughly test every product in application.

Liebert Australia has been honoured by other Liebert international operations that have adopted its designs and technology. The US-based parent company used the design and technology of the Australian operations when it set up plants in India. Although Liebert Australia is one of the international company's smaller subsidiaries, it is still a very profitable operation.

Supporting Customers

The company's service division, Liebert Global Services (LGS), is unparalleled in the industry, and provides support ranging from technical advice given over the telephone to hands-on oversight and management of multiple sites throughout the world.

LGS's Customer Response Centre provides both rapid response and emergency service, as well as support, for Liebert equipment 24 hours a day, 365 days a year. Liebert's key objective is to keep clients' vital systems operating.

Liebert enjoys a good retention rate, with many staff members who have remained with the company for up to 20 years. Employees take pride in their craftsmanship, working in a team-based culture to manufacture a high-quality product. Reflecting Sydney's multicultural population, Liebert's workers represent many cultures from around the globe.

Community and Industry Involvement

Liebert Australia is a consistent sponsor of worthwhile charities and community programs. Donations, at both a corporate and an employee level, have helped raise funds for such needy causes as the New Children's Hospital, Westmead, and the Australian Kidney Foundation.

Liebert Corporation Australia is a founding member of the Australian Industry Group (AIG), a member of the American Chamber of Commerce in Australia, and a Certified Australian Government Supplier. Liebert's head office and manufacturing plant in Sydney also operate to ISO 9000 quality standards.

Total Solutions

Liebert is a total solutions provider. With a diverse product range and very highly skilled employees, Liebert Australia offers integrated solutions to clients' problems. Liebert Australia recognises the importance of building and maintaining a lasting partnership with clients.

Liebert meets the challenges of a changing technological world by constantly improving its systems to meet the constantly changing needs of its customers. Spurred by its motto, "Liebert . . . keeping business in business", the company develops innovative solutions with a range of diverse products to make emerging niche markets its own. Driven by its dedication to its customers and its research and development, Liebert's technological leadership in precision environmental and power protection systems is certain to continue well into the next millennium.

LIEBERT MEETS THE CHALLENGES OF A CHANGING TECHNOLOGICAL WORLD BY CONSTANTLY IMPROVING ITS SYSTEMS TO MEET THE CONSTANTLY CHANGING NEEDS OF ITS CUSTOMERS.

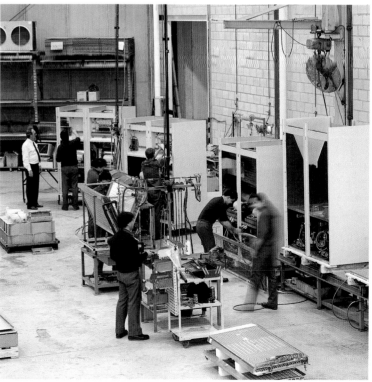

Corporate Relocations

MARGARET KELLY PIONEERED IN AUSTRALIA THE FIRST PRO-fessional commercial relocation service for executives when she established her relocation company in 1983. Corporate Relocations is dedicated to increasing the immediate productivity and effectiveness of the relocating executive and enhancing the lives and wellbeing of their families. Kelly identified the need for the service from

personal experience. As an executive with a major advertising company, she was relocated to Johannesburg. Scheduled to work from the first day of her arrival, she found it frustrating and unproductive to simultaneously work, find accommodation, and settle gracefully into her new surroundings. Upon her return to Sydney in 1983, Kelly decided to start her own business to help executives relocate efficiently and successfully. Her key to success was to offer a service of unsurpassable quality within a cost-effective budget.

Setting Up

Kelly grew her new enterprise by first building a database of potential customers from her first-hand knowledge of the business world, especially in Sydney and Melbourne. Applying her marketing strategy with a disciplined approach, she then made a list of companies that she knew regularly relocated senior staff. The list was expanded by checking through the telephone directory for companies she sensed would regularly relocate staff. After writing to the companies, Kelly personally telephoned everyone to whom she had written. She contacted 100 companies each week and found that most of them appreciated the issue because of their own unsuccessful relocation efforts.

Corporate Relocations' first client, Shell, was so impressed with the service that it recommended

Kelly's company to its accounting firm. Success soon attracted the attention of the media, and the *Sydney Morning Herald*, *Business Review Weekly*, and the *Financial Review*—some of Australia's most respected publications—carried articles about Corporate Relocations.

In the late 1990s, Corporate Relocations conducted a survey of its own customers and those of its competitors. Kelly is proud that all respondents viewed Corporate Relocations as the premium service provider. "We were seen as the most quality-driven company, even by companies that didn't use us," she says.

Service through Experience

At the heart of Corporate Relocations' services are experienced consultants who listen carefully to people in order to better understand their relocation needs. With experience behind them, the consultants organise all necessary practicalities to effect a quick and efficient relocation.

Consultants counsel clients about any discrepancies between expectations and likely outcomes. Corporate Relocations' education consultant assists in choosing the most appropriate schools for children. A detailed profile of the new community helps executives and their families settle into a new home and location quickly. Beyond the physical relocation, Corporate Relocations helps with the psychological aspects, offering support in building a network of friends.

Flexibility is a hallmark of Corporate Relocations' services. With its Comprehensive Service Program, Corporate Relocations covers and organises every possible detail of the transfer. With its other programs,

MARGARET KELLY PIONEERED IN AUSTRALIA THE FIRST PROFESSIONAL COMMERCIAL RELOCATION SERVICE FOR EXECUTIVES WHEN SHE ESTABLISHED CORPORATE RELOCATIONS

EDUCATION IS A KEY DRIVER IN ANY RELOCATION INVOLVING SCHOOL-AGE CHILDREN. A CORPORATE RELOCATIONS EDUCATION CONSULTANT IS AVAILABLE TO ADVISE AND MAKE APPLICATION TO APPROPRIATE SCHOOLS.

the company tailors a relocation strategy for the client's individual needs and interests.

Worldwide Growth

Today, Corporate Relocations has a network of associates in New Zealand, Europe, South Africa, Asia, and the United States. Kelly continues to pioneer innovations in the industry that she launched. Taking advantage of the latest technology, Corporate Relocations became in 1996 the first company in the Australian relocation industry to build a Web site.

For Kelly, the challenge in growing a business is maintaining integrity. Corporate Relocations made a strategic decision not to grow through expanding its volume of business, but rather by completing a quality relocation every time. "We take enormous pride in what we do," says Kelly.

Corporate Relocations' staff is its primary asset, giving the company its competitive edge. Kelly employs people who have knowledge of the world, good communication skills, and empathy for the situations clients must face in relocations. Regular training keeps staff members current in relevant fields, such as migration and cross-cultural studies.

A significant quality that sets Corporate Relocations apart from competitors is that it does not accept commissions or incentives from its service providers. The company says this frees it to make recommendations that suit only the client. "We don't work with companies that have a cookie cutter mentality about their employees. We work only with companies that value their people. Our competitive edge is that we value the employees that are valued by their companies," says Kelly.

Kelly is proud that she began an industry that is now large enough to have growing niche markets and that her company remains the premier industry operator. Corporate Relocations intends to maintain its leadership position while continuing its growth and taking pride in what it does best: relocating executives successfully.

A HARBOUR VIEW COMMANDS A PREMIUM RENTAL IN SYDNEY.

FedEx

FEDEX VANS TRAVELLING THROUGHOUT SYDNEY'S BUSINESS community are as common on the busy streets as ferries on the great city's scenic harbour. In just 10 years since FedEx established operations in Sydney, the company has become a clearly recognised entity within Australian business sectors and a strong competitor to the existing leaders in the Australian air freight industry. After FedEx cemented its

presence within Sydney in 1989, its coverage across Australia grew quickly and facilities were opened in all major cities. Since beginning its Australian network, FedEx has introduced a number of developments to help the company gain a bigger slice of the international air express market and secure the company's stronghold on the Australian market. These include the choreographed opening of new facilities that cater to increased demand for FedEx services, the launch of the company's five weekly flights into Australia as part of FedEx's AsiaOne® network, and the consolidation of the company's Sydney-based head office and warehouse into a single location to better serve customers.

Why Sydney?

Sydney is the commercial capital of Australia and represents the largest market in the country. Most key exporting organisations are headquartered in Sydney or have established facilities based there. The city's Kingsford Smith Airport is Australia's largest airport in terms of servicing both commuters and freight.

In June 1998, FedEx opened a new regional facility in Sydney in response to increased demand for time-definite express services from businesses in the city's western and southwestern suburbs. With its central location, the new operation in Rydalmere is close to the geographic heart of metropolitan Sydney, making it easily accessible to businesses in the city's fast-growing commercial districts and providing customers with even quicker access to the company's global express network through the new facility.

FedEx currently employs approximately 360 people nationwide and boasts a fleet more than 75 vehicles. Its principal officer—Managing Director, Australia Bruce Myers—is based in Sydney.

Worldwide Flight

In September 1998, FedEx became the first express transportation company operating in Sydney to launch scheduled express air freight services between Australia and destinations in Asia and the rest of the world using its own aircraft. This development marks a significant milestone in Australia not only for FedEx and its customers, but also for aviation and air freight history.

The FedEx AsiaOne® network connects five weekly flights originating in the United States that depart from Memphis and arrive in Sydney via Honolulu. From Sydney, the flights head north to Subic Bay, FedEx's Asia-Pacific hub. This connectivity allows Australian customers to enjoy improved delivery times of 24 to 48 hours for inbound shipments, and later cut-off times for outbound packages. The use of FedEx's dedicated aircraft allows packages of virtually any weight to be shipped with increased flexibility. Essentially, the FedEx AsiaOne® network has established the company as the Australian export market's express gateway to Asia and the world.

In 1999, FedEx announced the consolidation and relocation of its two Sydney headquarters to Sydney Business Centre at Alexandria. The 10,000-square-metre space comprises 6,900 square metres of warehouse and 3,000 square metres of office space. The new location—a short distance from Sydney's Kingsford Smith Airport—has brought together the company's operational teams, allowing FedEx to develop new and improved ways to service its customer base faster and more effectively.

FEDEX IS THE FIRST AND ONLY EXPRESS TRANSPORTATION COMPANY IN AUSTRALIA TO OPERATE DEDICATED SERVICES ON ITS OWN AIRCRAFT TO ASIAN DESTINATIONS AND THE WORLD. THE MD-11, AN EFFICIENT, RELIABLE AIRCRAFT WELL SUITED TO INTERNATIONAL FLYING, IS FREQUENTLY USED ON THE AUSTRALIAN ROUTES.

THE SYDNEY OFFICE OF MICHAEL PAGE INTERNATIONAL IS proud of its success. The pre-eminent specialist recruitment company established its Sydney office in 1985, and today, it has a staff of more than 100 consultants. Michael Page in Sydney is a division of Michael Page International, which was established in 1976 in the United Kingdom, and today has offices in Hong Kong, Singapore, New Zealand, Europe, and the United States.

The parent company, Interim Services Inc., places more than 400,000 people each year, making it one of the largest recruitment companies in the world. With headquarters located in Fort Lauderdale, Interim Services has more than 700 offices throughout the Asia Pacific region, Europe, and North America.

Specialist Teams

Within the Sydney office, specialist teams cover two of the primary employment fields served by the firm: Michael Page Technology and Michael Page Sales & Marketing.

Michael Page Technology, launched in 1994, handles information technology (IT) job placements for all positions—permanent or contract—across all industry sectors (i.e. banking and finance, IT and telecommunications, consultancies, and general commerce). The positions range from junior help desk roles to IT directorships, including systems engineers, analyst programmers, and business analysts. As a specialist recruitment organisation across a wide breadth of the technology sector (and in such competitive times), Michael Page Technology has the advantage of being part of an international group with consultants with professional, degree-qualified backgrounds working in a non-commissioned, team-focused environment.

Established in 1993, Michael Page Sales & Marketing is designed to service the sales and marketing sector, covering positions from sales assistant to product manager to director. Through its knowledge of the market, Michael Page Sales & Marketing identified the need for a service to recruit temporary sales and marketing positions for non-strategic work on short-term projects, and has expanded rapidly in this area over the last couple of years. In addition, Michael Page Sales & Marketing has developed particular expertise in the IT, financial services, consumer, and media/entertainment industry sectors, in both permanent and temporary placements.

Culture of Success

Michael Page has built its unique corporate culture through teams that consist of specialist consultants who work on a non-commission basis. Working in teams with the interest of the client being paramount, staff develop long-term relationships and share critical information that makes for successful placements. Michael Page's consultants specialise in the different employment sectors—their industries, salary levels, and permanent and contract work. Consultants track emerging activity in the market to offer clients a comprehensive service that is rich in fact, up to date, and flexible.

The company's rigorous monitoring program evaluates each and every assignment through confidential feedback that invites frank comments from clients and candidates. Networking (between the company, employers, and prospective employment candidates) is enhanced by the company's marketing activities, which include seminars, business breakfasts, boardroom briefings, and other industry events.

Good Citizen

Michael Page donates a portion of its earnings to several charities in the community. Recent beneficiaries have included the Garvan Research Foundation and the Guide Dogs Association. The Make-A-Wish Foundation, established to make critically ill children's dreams come true, receives at Christmas the money that Michael Page saves by not sending expensive, customised Christmas cards.

With success sustained by a unique corporate culture, Michael Page maintains its pre-eminent position in recruitment in Sydney and throughout the world. The company will continue to develop creative solutions for matching candidates and employers in a rapidly changing marketplace.

AMANDA PERILLE SERVES AS DIRECTOR OF MICHAEL PAGE SALES & MARKETING AND TECHNOLOGY DIVISIONS IN SYDNEY.

*U*NITED AIRLINES IS A GLOBAL AIRLINE THAT IS RISING TO THE challenge of the next century by listening to its customers and meeting their needs. United is the world's largest airline, operating some 2,300 flights per day, carrying nearly 250,000 passengers to over 220 destinations in more than 30 countries. United serves both the business and the leisure traveller, as well as cargo service markets, on five

continents. In addition, United is one of the world's largest international carriers, flying nearly 9 million travellers on 70,000 international flights per year.

United Airlines in Sydney

In Sydney, United employs 200 people and carries 120,000 passengers out of Australia per year. The airline's routes include nonstop flights to the United States, with an excellent US network to carry people beyond the west coast. In addition, United is a member of the Olympic Airline Team, which is an official sponsor of the Sydney 2000 Olympics.

United's Concierge Service provides personal attention and is able to cater to the customer's every need. This service also provides priority services during irregular operations, as well as assistance in customs, immigration, and baggage collection.

The airline's Valet Departures Service offers an alternative to airport car parking for those who drive to the airport through the Sheraton in Sydney. While flight check-in is made at the United counter in the hotel, the traveller's car is parked by a valet in a secure location, and a shuttle bus will take the passenger to the airport.

United also has a Red Carpet Club at Sydney Airport. The airline's Red Carpet Clubs have proven themselves to be both business facilities and refreshment areas in a quiet atmosphere within the airport. The Red Carpet lounge is the largest lounge facility at Sydney Airport, and admission is paid by annual membership or is complimentary if flying United First or United Business Class.

Aviation History

For more than 70 years, United has had a history of leadership and innovations that include the world's first flight attendant service in 1930, the first airline flight kitchen in 1936, the first nonstop coast-to-coast US flight in 1955, and the first nationwide automated reservations system in 1971.

United first took off in 1926 as Varney Air Lines, a mail carrier in

UNITED SERVES BOTH THE BUSINESS AND THE LEISURE TRAVELLER, AS WELL AS CARGO SERVICE MARKETS ON FIVE CONTINENTS. IN SYDNEY, UNITED CARRIES 120,000 PASSENGERS OUT OF AUSTRALIA PER YEAR.

the Pacific Northwest. In 1927, Chicago became the key midpoint for travel between San Francisco and New York for the carriers National Air Transport and Boeing Air Transport. In the 1930s, these airlines, along with Pacific Air Transport and Varney, combined to become United.

In 1990, United became the first commercial carrier to use satellite data communications in flight, allowing air traffic controllers and pilots to know where planes are at all times, even over the Pacific Ocean. This clear, quick, and uninterrupted communication is done directly between the cockpit and ground controllers, and is used instead of radio signals.

United is proud of its safety record and is a carrier known throughout the industry for making air traffic safer. Ongoing efforts include the development of safety programs that have been adopted by other carriers such as windshear training for pilots, human factors or teamwork training, air-to-ground radio navigation, and de-icing.

Star Alliance
Star Alliance is a global air network offering customers convenient worldwide service through global recognition, coordinated schedules, interairport check-in, and the most convenient access to more than 720 destinations worldwide. Customers of each of the participating airlines may accrue mileage redeemable on all carriers within the Star Alliance. In addition, qualified customers enjoy reciprocal privileges at Star Alliance airport lounges around the world and also may apply their accumulated mileage toward elite status programs with Star Alliance member airlines. United, together with Ansett Australia, Air New Zealand, Thai Airways, Air Canada, Lufthansa, SAS, Varig, and All Nippon Airways, are members of the Star Alliance, the world's first truly global airline alliance.

Customer Satisfaction
During an exhaustive air traveller study, United discovered that the US airline industry was failing to meet the expectations and needs of its customers. In response, United developed a customer-driven initiative that would revolutionise its service and the industry. In addition to the basic elements of safety, reliability, and competitive prices, United's core

customer-satisfaction philosophy includes providing genuine attention to each traveller's needs, offering comfort as the minimum experience and enjoyment as the ideal, global access, reward and recognition, and candour and responsibility.

Based on its customers' responses, United is currently investing $391 million to improve airport communications and check-in procedures. United's numerous product and service initiatives run the gamut of the airline's operations, ranging from new, more timely, and candid delay announcements to improving the comfort of all 60,000 seats in its fleet.

E-Ticket[SM] Worldwide
Electronic ticketing (E-Ticket) offers the ultimate in ease and convenience.

United's reservation system helps reservation agents and travel agents serve customers better, and makes flight information accessible. Travellers do not have to worry about lost or stolen tickets, and there is no waiting for the arrival of tickets.

Ticket/boarding passes are easily printed at check-in. Purchase, refund, exchange, and itinerary changes are all available over the phone 24 hours a day. To date, more than 25 million customers have enjoyed the benefits that E-Tickets have to offer.

United's Web site—which can be found at www.ual.com—was the first to provide real-time pricing of mileage, a flight mileage calculator, online enrolment, and change-of-address processing.

Hotel Nikko Darling Harbour/Sydney

As the Australian flagship property of Nikko Hotels International, the Hotel Nikko Darling Harbour/Sydney is distinguished by its location and the success it has enjoyed since first opening in 1991. With 645 rooms, including 56 suites, Australia's largest hotel projects an elegant and streamlined profile against the Sydney cityscape. The Hotel Nikko's location on the eastern shore of Darling Harbour, adjacent to the central business district, provides immediate access along a private walkway to the renowned Sydney Aquarium, as well as wharves for harbour cruise boats. This environment served as the inspiration for the hotel's nautical architectural theme, which is reminiscent of a stately 1920s ocean liner.

Tokyo-based Nikko Hotels International was established in 1970 as a subsidiary of Japan Airlines Company. Nearly three decades later, the chain straddles the world, with 50 hotels in 17 countries, and expects to double its number of properties by 2001.

The Heart of the City

Views from the Hotel Nikko's 15 stories take in not only the colour and life of the harbour, but also the excitement of the city. The central business district—acknowledged as the national and regional corporate capital—is a stroll away, as is the prestigious Queen Victoria Building shopping complex and other shopping attractions. Vibrant Chinatown is located three blocks south, and the Sydney Harbour Casino is a five-minute ride away.

Each year, 15 million people visit Darling Harbour, a major urban redevelopment that opened in 1988. In addition to large convention and exhibition facilities, the harbour's attractions include an IMAX cinema, the National Maritime Museum, and the Chinese Garden, as well as a green oasis with park benches and a duck pond.

General Manager Fumio Moroi explains that the hotel's philosophy and level of service reflect a shift in the market since the property welcomed its first guests. "When the chain opened, certain hotels were catering just to groups, but now we're trying to focus on the local market, as well as the European and American markets."

Building on 15 years of experience with the Nikko chain, Moroi plans to achieve an increase in the number of individual guests from 17 per cent to between 30 and 35 per cent. He is also developing the hotel's profile in order to increase its share of convention attendees and attract more of the traffic between Melbourne and Sydney.

All guests are treated to traditional Japanese hospitality, in which the host proffers to the guest a warm towel, known as *o-shibori*, to refresh the hands and face. "Our concept of establishing a good relationship with guests means greeting them at the door with *o-shibori* and then accompanying them to their rooms," says Moroi. In order to realise this level of service, the Hotel Nikko has developed the unique concept of guest relations managers. These dedicated staff members are assigned to greet individual guests and update records about their preferences in accommodations, food, and other hotel services. When patrons arrive on subsequent visits, their wishes can be anticipated, thus enhancing their stay at the hotel.

Award-Winning Accommodations

In 1997, the Hotel Nikko Darling Harbour was a finalist in the Best Five-Star Tourism Accommodation Awards presented by the Australian Hotels Association (NSW). The most exclusive accommodations are found in the Presidential Suite, which boasts

THE HOTEL NIKKO DARLING HARBOUR, AUSTRALIA'S LARGEST HOTEL, PROJECTS AN ELEGANT AND STREAMLINED PROFILE AGAINST THE SYDNEY CITYSCAPE.

INNOVATIVE CUISINE IS ANOTHER
HALLMARK OF THE HOTEL NIKKO
DARLING HARBOUR. PERHAPS MOST
EXCITING HAS BEEN THE INTRODUC-
TION OF PACIFIC RIM CUISINE AT THE
[illegible] [illegible] [illegible] [illegible].

an office, a second bedroom, and generously sized dining and lounge spaces. Guests can also choose the hotel's Nikko Floors, which offer personalised service, access to a private lounge with adjoining conference room, and a variety of local and international business publications.

Business guests have access to a battery of special amenities, ranging from a personal computer to full secretarial services. Four business suites and a boardroom accommodate conferences, meetings, seminars, and a variety of other gatherings, while the Grand Ballroom suits major events such as formal dinners. On request, the hotel can supply any equipment or service needed to complete a business activity.

A gallery of exclusive shops—including specialty gift emporiums, a Cartier boutique, and the exclusive Japanese department store Takashimaya—are housed in the heritage-listed Corn Exchange Building portion of the property. Built in 1887, the old sandstone warehouse was embraced in the hotel's design, as were several other historic structures.

Culinary Innovations

Innovative cuisine is another hallmark of the Hotel Nikko Darling Harbour. Perhaps most exciting has been the introduction of Pacific Rim cuisine at the award-winning Corn

Exchange. "It's a unique, health oriented approach to food, based on a mixture of the cuisine of the countries around the rim of the Pacific Ocean," says Moroi.

In addition, the Kamogawa Restaurant serves authentic Japanese delicacies in an elegant and traditional setting. Guests can also mix with locals at the Dundee Arms Pub—the fourth oldest in Sydney—which offers counter lunches, along with beer from local boutique brewers. Even the hotel's wine list has a spe-

cial focus. "We highlight Australian wine, which I think is much better than the wine produced anywhere in the world except France and Italy," says Moroi.

Whether they're eating, sleeping, meeting, or just relaxing, guests at the Hotel Nikko experience personalised service from the moment they check in. With Hotel Nikko's history of enhanced service and its ideal waterfront location, the future augurs well for this five-star jewel on Darling Harbour.

VIEWS FROM THE HOTEL NIKKO'S
15 STORIES TAKE IN NOT ONLY THE
COLOUR AND LIFE OF THE HARBOUR,
BUT ALSO THE EXCITEMENT OF THE
CITY.

COMPUTER ASSOCIATES INTERNATIONAL, INC. (CA), WITH headquarters in Islandia, New York, is the world leader in mission-critical business software. The company develops, licenses, and supports more than 500 integrated products that include enterprise computing and information management, application development, manufacturing, and financial applications. CA's Global Professional Services

oganisation provides consulting, education, and implementation services. CA has more than 14,000 people in 160 offices in 43 countries, and had revenue of US$5.3 billion in fiscal year 1999. The company's Web site can be found at www.cai.com.

In Australia, CA's first office was established in Sydney in 1984. Since then, the company's success has resulted in the opening of other Australian offices in Melbourne, Adelaide, Brisbane, Perth, and Canberra. In New Zealand, CA has offices in Auckland and Wellington. Under the leadership of Managing Director John Ruthven, the company's operations in Australia and New Zealand have a collective staff that now totals more than 600, and

the company is ISO 9002 quality assured. In addition, CA Australia is a foundation member of the Australian Federal Government's Partnership for Development Program (PDP).

Five-Pronged Business Strategy
Computer Associates' management pursues a five-pronged growth strategy. The key points of this market-driven strategy are professional services, internal product development, targeted acquisitions of complementary technology, effective integration of new products, and the leveraging of key partnerships.

There are four software categories at Computer Associates that deliver the infrastructure that enables the business to fulfill its strategic goals.

Enterprise Management Software
Today's business computing environments are highly complex and increasingly diverse. Companies typically have hardware from multiple vendors running on various operating systems using many brands of software. Adding to the confusion, much of this equipment is generally linked through a network, as well as via the Internet or intranet connections.

CA creates innovative software solutions to manage these complex computing environments while maintaining a high level of efficiency, reliability, and security in networked computing environments. Unicenter–CA's flagship client/server product–was the first software to offer effective, comprehensive, multiplatform management.

Next-Generation Software
The release of Unicenter TNG, the next generation of the popular Unicenter product, raises information technology management to an entirely new level. Unicenter TNG links all aspects of a company's computing infrastructure–across different platforms, facilities, and continents–to provide a complete picture of macro-

JOHN RUTHVEN IS MANAGING DIRECTOR OF COMPUTER ASSOCIATES INTERNATIONAL, INC.

THE RELEASE OF COMPUTER ASSOCIATES' UNICENTER TNG, THE NEXT GENERATION OF THE COMPANY'S POPULAR UNICENTER PRODUCT, RAISES INFORMATION TECHNOLOGY MANAGEMENT TO AN ENTIRELY NEW LEVEL.

business processes. The software's revolutionary real-world interface uses 3-D technology and animation to display the entire computing environment, allowing users to navigate through the enterprise intuitively.

New Dimension with Unicenter
CA takes the next generation into a new dimension with Unicenter TND. This will allow customers to anticipate problems and fix them before they occur instead of just reacting to them. Its neural network capability collects and analyses historical data to identify patterns that might predict problems and failures.

In an in-house testing of Unicenter TND, the system warned operators that one of the company's servers was about to go down. The warning gave CA staff enough time to find the problem and fix it before it failed.

Information Management
CA's award-winning database and application development tools continue to be the standard against which others are measured. By leveraging the benefits of object-oriented technology and the untapped market resources of the Internet, CA's Jasmine and Ingres II allow businesses to build and deploy real-world business applications. These applications are designed for conducting electronic commerce quickly and easily on the World Wide Web.

Jasmine and Ingres II, the Internet Commerce Enabled database, are both setting precedents for the industry to follow. With this new generation of technology, clients can protect their legacy systems investments while they exploit emerging information technologies.

Manufacturing and Distribution Software
From single-plant manufacturing, to worldwide distribution networks, CA is the world's leading provider of manufacturing and distribution software. By combining processing elements from financial management, distributing, and manufacturing into a single, integrated, enterprise-wide system, CA's manufacturing and distribution software meets the broadest range of corporate needs.

Financial Software
CA offers a vast range of financial and banking software products. From the simple, single-business, entry-level program, through leading high-end accounting software, CA offers ACCPAC. For Fortune 1,000 companies requiring multinational, multi-currency, financial software, CA offers Masterpiece/Net.

Today, more than 74,000 clients use CA financial software on virtually every major hardware platform, from PCs to mainframe computers, making CA the world's largest provider of financial software products.

Global Professional Services
In response to the growing customer demand for the total solution to be provided and implemented by the same supplier, CA formed Global Professional Services (GPS). Operating with the vast resources of a global organisation, GPS targets solutions at a local level by managing projects from local CA offices rather than remote offices.

CA's diverse consultant base enriches its teams with a variety of backgrounds and perspectives that broaden the scope of the company's solution development. Aligned with CA's array of business partnerships, this diversity offers a significant set of resources to further boost clients' competitive advantage.

Creating Everyday Miracles
As part of CA's commitment of giving back to the community, Computer Associates Australia is the principal corporate sponsor of the Cranio Facial Foundation (CFF), the first national organisation dedicated to the charitable delivery of craniofacial surgery.

Headed by David David, Australia's 23-year-old Cranio Facial Unit in Adelaide pioneered a multidisciplinary model for treating craniofacial patients who have been grossly disfigured at birth or by trauma. The CFF has long been recognised by Australia's federal government as a centre of excellence.

Child-Care Facilities
CA Australia is the first subsidiary outside the United States to benefit from CA's policy to roll out internationally on-site child-care facilities at CA premises. This on-site child-care capability is believed to be only the second such employee child-care centre in Australia.

CA'S OPAL IS AN ADVANCED MULTIMEDIA USER INTERFACE, WITH FLEXIBLE DEPLOYMENT AND POWERFUL INTEGRATION. JASMINE TND USES CUTTINGEDGE TECHNOLOGIES, EXISTING DATA, AND LOGIC TO QUICKLY BUILD, DEPLOY, AND MANAGE A NEW GENERATION OF INTELLIGENT E-BUSINESS SOLUTIONS.

Sydney Marriott Hotel

SYDNEY, A CITY OF GENUINE WORLD-CLASS PROPORTIONS, IS A unique location blessed with breathtaking natural beauty and man-made icons recognised anywhere around the globe—spectacular Sydney Harbour, Darling Harbour, Hyde Park, Harbour Bridge, and Sydney Opera House. ᔕᕽ Culturally diverse, Sydney sets the standard as Australia's largest city with international shopping, dining, leisure, and

THE SYDNEY MARRIOTT HOTEL BOASTS 241 SPACIOUS GUESTROOMS AND 14 SUITES, ALL OF WHICH ARE WELL APPOINTED (LEFT).

FROM THE WARMTH OF THE FIRST WELCOME AND UNTIL THEY LEAVE, GUESTS AT THE SYDNEY MARRIOTT ARE GIVEN COMPLETE ATTENTION IN EVERY DETAIL (RIGHT).

sporting facilities. Sydney is widely accepted as the social, financial, cultural, and business heart of the nation—a city that sits comfortably in comparison with any one of the great cities of the world.

When visitors stay at Sydney Marriott Hotel—located on picturesque Hyde Park on the fringe of the central business district—they are geographically in the real heart of Sydney and are perfectly positioned to access everything Sydney has to offer. The hotel is 25 minutes away from the domestic and international airports, and 10 minutes from Sydney Harbour, Circular Quay, the Rocks, the casino, Darling Harbour, the retail centre, Kings Cross, diverse restaurant options, night-life, and government and financial districts.

The Sydney Marriott boasts 241 spacious guestrooms and 14 suites, all of which are well appointed to offer every facility expected by discerning guests. For the comfort of all, the hotel provides nonsmoking rooms. From the warmth of the first welcome and until they leave, guests are given complete attention in every detail, large or small, from the hotel's staff. For business or pleasure, visitors can be assured of the ultimate in both comfort and service.

"I think the ambience of the hotel is created not just by the decor, but also by the staff and their attention to detail. Their caring captures the spirit to serve, which is what Marriott is all about," says Ken Edwards, the hotel's general manager. "The staff works with management as a team. We don't use the word 'I'; we use 'team,' " explains Edwards. "My philosophy is that I give people ownership. Ownership becomes responsibility. They operate their departments accordingly, and my role is one of custodian. I advise them and I help them. At the end of the day, I don't run the hotel—my managers and my staff run the hotel."

In the style of the local Paddington Cafe Society, the Park Bench Cafe is a relaxing venue for morning coffee, a light lunch, or a leisurely afternoon tea. With busy feet and passing traffic, the Sydney business day passes before one's eyes when looking across to the calming oasis of Hyde Park.

There's no better place to break from the more formal hours of the day than Windows on the Park. The à la carte lunchtime menu offers contemporary Australian cuisine. As night-time beckons and Hyde Park lights up, the restaurant offers casual, elegant dining with a special ambience. And when the daily pressures ease, Archibalds Cocktail Bar is the perfect place to unwind and partake in the timeless art of con-

versation. Whether for predinner cocktails or a nightcap, clients and friends often rendezvous at Archibalds.

For the corporate traveller, the Sydney Marriott has every need covered. Spacious guestrooms are equipped with the dedicated services of fax/modem connections, voice mail, 24-hour room service and news service, and a work desk. Internet and email facilities are available through the hotel's Business Centre, and the Marriott's Executive Level provides private corporate facilities and a lounge.

The hotel's enviable position on Hyde Park provides superb natural light and an ambience that might be the key ingredient to a successful conference or meeting. The Marriott's flexible room options can accommo-date up to 280 guests, and the hotel can tailor a venue to individual needs, whatever the occasion.

When business turns to leisure of the exercise kind, the Marriott is once again perfectly located. Guests may walk or jog through Hyde Park to the Domain, the Royal Botanic Gardens, and the harbour. Upon their return, they may enjoy the facilities of the hotel's rooftop recreational deck, swimming pool, gym, sauna, and spa, as well as the magnificent views of the sensational Sydney skyline and Hyde Park below.

"We believe that when you're comfortable, you can do anything," says Edwards. "And you can do any thing when you stay at the heart of this unforgettable city, the Sydney Marriott Hotel."

Compuware Asia-Pacific Pty Ltd

COMPUWARE, A LEADING PROVIDER OF SOFTWARE PRODUCTS and professional services to many of the world's largest information technology (IT) organisations, has had a presence in Australia since 1980. Compuware Asia-Pacific Pty Ltd was established in Sydney in 1994, when its parent, Compuware Corporation, bought back the company's Australian distributorship. John Debrincat, who had been a director of

CLOCKWISE FROM TOP RIGHT: COMPUWARE'S REGIONAL HEADQUARTERS—NORTH SYDNEY, NEW SOUTH WALES

PETER PRITCHARD, MARKETING DIRECTOR, COMPUWARE ASIA-PACIFIC, MEETS WITH AN ANSETT INTERNATIONAL AIR FREIGHT REPRESENTATIVE AT MASCOT AIRPORT.

THE COMPUWARE MARKETING TEAM MEETS WITH JULIAN CHURCHMAN, CREATIVE DIRECTOR-SPIRE DESIGN CONSULTANTS, TO DISCUSS AN UPCOMING MARKETING CAMPAIGN.

JOHN DEBRINCAT, VICE-PRESIDENT AND GROUP MANAGING DIRECTOR, COMPUWARE ASIA-PACIFIC

Executive Computing, took up the vice-presidency of the new operation.

The company's mission is to be the best worldwide provider of quality software products and services designed to increase productivity, continue creating practical solutions that meet changing needs, and surpass customers' expectations.

Sydney Headquarters

Compuware Asia-Pacific is headquartered in North Sydney, the hub of the IT industry in Australia. "I decided to set up our headquarters in Sydney because it is the leading IT city in the region," says Debrincat. "It has a stable political climate, a strong technical infrastructure, and a large pool of experienced IT professionals that we required for our expansion."

Debrincat has been the driving force behind the success of the operation. From a single office in Sydney with a staff of 30, Compuware Asia-Pacific today employs 200 people, with branch offices in Melbourne, Brisbane, Canberra, Singapore, Hong Kong, and Beijing.

The vision of Compuware Corporation's founding fathers has remained unchanged over the decades. Thomas Thewes and Allen Cutting, along with current Chairman and CEO Peter Karmanos Jr., established the organisation in Detroit in 1972 to help other companies master their IT systems and succeed in their areas of expertise.

Compuware has since grown through mergers and acquisitions, as well as by actively acquiring and

integrating proven technology from established vendors. Both locally and worldwide, the company nurtures partnerships and alliances with most of the world's major IT enterprises, including IBM. The Corporate Alliances unit, for example, manages the commercial and technical relationships that Compuware maintains with leading IT providers.

Compuware is today the fifth-largest independent software company, and one of the largest professional

services organisations, in the world. Additionally, *Business Week*, the premier international business publication, recently ranked Compuware seventh in financial strength among high-tech companies worldwide.

Expertise

As the IT industry has moved from heavy mainframe systems to a mixture of mainframe and client/server technology, Compuware has shifted its focus toward providing practical and cost-effective solutions for clients. Because many businesses rely heavily on applications for their survival in order to maintain a competitive edge, Compuware has responded by doing all it can to ensure that those applications run efficiently and effectively. The company's business model falls naturally into four main areas: building, testing, managing, and deploying applications.

One of Compuware's leading IT solution systems is the UNIFACE application assembly environment, which allows large users to successfully implement changes to a system as technology upgrades are introduced. The system is based on a strategic framework that embraces the three primary elements that shape most applications: model-driven development, infrastructure independent deployment, and value added delivery. UNIFACE enables the construction and deployment of component-based applications for distributed environments, including the Internet. Recognised by the GartnerGroup as a leader in enterprise application development, Compuware's model-driven approach to programming combined with the ability to reuse in-house components, as well as components from other vendors— makes UNIFACE the ideal development tool.

Since the 1970s, organisations have relied on ad hoc tests before releasing software applications, often asking end users to perform product trials under field conditions. Compuware brings a structured approach to testing, with products that test the whole computing spectrum, from mainframe to PC, from OS/390 to Windows, and from localised systems to systems that span countries.

Once an application has been built, tested, and implemented in daily use, Compuware's EcoSYSTEM products ensure that those applica-

tions continue to run as required. EcoTOOLS measures and manages the health of the back end server hardware and the underlying database. EcoSCOPE constantly monitors application traffic across the network, notifying technical personnel if response times exceed preset limits or if other out-of-bounds conditions occur that would impact the users' applications. EcoSNAP manages failures that occur on the desktop, allowing users to continue processing, if possible, and notifying the business's help desk if there is a total failure.

Compuware's Professional Services Division uses its specialised knowledge to help organisations implement new systems or upgrade older legacy applications. The company has one of the largest product knowledge banks in the world, designed to be accessible to Compuware staff and their clients—anywhere, anytime.

Unique Service

Whether it's a large corporation or the smallest single-person business, Compuware earns clients' trust and respect by delivering quality service.

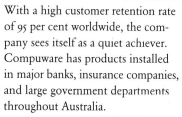

With a high customer retention rate of 95 per cent worldwide, the company sees itself as a quiet achiever. Compuware has products installed in major banks, insurance companies, and large government departments throughout Australia.

The company's guiding principles are enshrined in the performance standards set for all employees, and they create a common bond of trust that serves as the foundation for teamwork and the Compuware spirit. Clients are allocated a team of experts with a team leader, who acts as a coordinator of all necessary technical and administrative functions. Each assignment is approached with enthusiasm, and client relationships are based on integrity, creativity, and diligence.

As a significant force in Australian IT, Compuware Asia-Pacific is a dependable contributor to the nation's economic and technical development. Companies have come to depend on Compuware to keep their businesses up and running. Choosing this global firm for their critical business applications and solutions.

CLOCKWISE FROM TOP LEFT: COMPUWARE HAS ONE OF THE LARGEST PRODUCT KNOWLEDGE BANKS IN THE WORLD. PICTURED HERE IS COMPUWARE'S PRODUCT TRAINING FACILITY.

Established in 1992 in Sydney with a staff of 30, Compuware Asia-Pacific today employs 200 people, with branch offices in Melbourne, Brisbane, Canberra, Singapore, Hong Kong, and Beijing.

PICTURED HERE (FROM LEFT) BILL MINNIECON AND VICKY SALISBURY OF WORLD VISION MEET WITH COMPUWARE'S PETER PRITCHARD AT THE WALKABOUT GALLERY IN NEWTON.

A COMPUWARE MEMBER OF STAFF LEAVES THE HEAD OFFICE TO VISIT CLIENTS.

THE NEW SOUTH WALES DEPARTMENT OF STATE AND REGIONAL Development is responsible for promoting and encouraging economic expansion in Australia's premier state and in its capital city, Sydney. The organisation offers a comprehensive package of services to assist existing businesses with expansion and to facilitate the entry of new businesses into the marketplace. The vision that guides the department is one of a

dynamic and growing economy that delivers sustainable jobs and an enhanced standard of living for the people of New South Wales.

As an important division of the New South Wales government, the Department of State and Regional Development's (DSRD) goal is to promote business and economic activity throughout New South Wales. The organisation plays a key role in business development on the regional, state, and national levels, as well as

in attracting business from overseas. Established in 1995, DSRD is headquartered in Sydney–Australia's major centre of finance and business–and has offices in Tokyo and London.

Its knowledge of government gives DSRD a competitive edge, enabling it to help clients manage their relationships with other government bodies in the most effective and beneficial way in order to expedite economic expansion and activity. The reputation of trust that DSRD has

gained cements the confidential relationship between the organisation and investors.

DSRD's staff consists of nearly 200 highly dedicated individuals, many of whom are experts in their respective fields. As more staff have come into the department from the private sector, small businesses, multinationals, and large businesses, DSRD's understanding of the needs of business has improved, making the department more efficient and effective.

Premier City, Premier State

With a gross state product of more than US$120 billion, New South Wales is a powerhouse within the Asia-Pacific region. Sydney serves as the business, administrative, and political capital of the state, having a population that is cosmopolitan, well educated, and highly skilled. Local residents share a down-to-earth attitude that welcomes change, competition, and fairness.

A combination of high-tech, education, mining, manufacturing,

NEW SOUTH WALES DEPARTMENT OF STATE AND REGIONAL DEVELOPMENT MANAGERS BRIEF OVERSEAS TRADE DELEGATES AT THE DEPARTMENT'S GROSVENOR PLACE TRADE AND INVESTMENT CENTRE (TOP).

MORE THAN 260 FOREIGN COMPANIES HAVE ESTABLISHED THEIR REGIONAL HEADQUARTERS IN SYDNEY, AND HALF OF AUSTRALIA'S AND NEW ZEALAND'S TOP 500 COMPANIES HAVE LOCATED THEIR HEADQUARTERS IN THE CITY (BOTTOM).

and agricultural activity makes for a strong and diversified state economy. Financial, property, and retail services account for four-fifths of Sydney's economic product. The city is headquarters to the nation's major financial institutions, including the Sydney Futures Exchange and the Reserve Bank. The share market is among the busiest in the Southern Hemisphere

More than 260 foreign companies have established their regional headquarters in Sydney, and half of Australia's and New Zealand's top 500 companies have located their headquarters in the city. Three out of four domestic and international banks are headquartered in Sydney, offering a full range of services to business, commerce, and industry

Specialty Divisions That Help Businesses

Of the DSRD's five major divisions, the Investment Division pinpoints opportunities for businesses seeking to invest in the state, and develops programs to promote the state as a secure and profitable business envi-

ronment. The division specialises in finding locations that are suitable for a particular business's investment dollars, and assists such companies in making applications for government approval of projects at any level. The division helps the investor navigate through government regulators. In addition, the DSRD will also help the investor identify additional avenues for business activity that may be associated with the project

The Trade and Business Services Division is dedicated to helping small- to medium-sized businesses become more competitive by pursuing export opportunities for their goods and services. The department provides key information on overseas markets and coordinates trade missions, among a variety of other support services.

The Regional Development Division has established 13 regional development boards, and works out of 18 offices. A package of services and programs identifies new markets with the aim of attracting industries to particular regions within the state. Programs bring together groups and

businesses with common interests in order to promote local development

Promoting links between business, research and development institutions, and the public and private sectors ensures that business development is boosted within and outside the state. The Industry Development Division coordinates a wide range of events and trade shows that build strong relationships among all such organisations and industries

The Policy and Resources Division initiates economic and industry studies to understand trends and developments in the state's economy. Based on this information, the division formulates advice and policies for the government in order to enhance business activity in the state. An essential function of this division is setting performance benchmarks for the state's business activity and economy.

The DSRD actively promotes Sydney and New South Wales as the fastest-growing commercial centre in the Asia-Pacific region. The department is proactive, analysing economic and business activities and trends so that it can develop effective services and programs to meet the needs of the community it serves and to strengthen the state's economy. Dedicated to making the vision of a dynamic and growing economy a reality, the New South Wales Department of State and Regional Development is an integral part of the Sydney community.

WITH A GROSS STATE PRODUCT OF MORE THAN US$180 BILLION, NEW SOUTH WALES IS A POWERHOUSE WITHIN THE ASIA-PACIFIC REGION. PICTURED HERE IS THE CENTRAL BUSINESS DISTRICT OF SYDNEY (TOP LEFT).

SYDNEY SERVES AS THE BUSINESS, ADMINISTRATIVE, AND POLITICAL CAPITAL OF NEW SOUTH WALES. PICTURED HERE IS AN AERIAL VIEW OF THE CITY AND ITS HARBOUR (TOP RIGHT).

MODERN OFFICE TOWERS OUTLINE THE EVER CHANGING SYDNEY SKYLINE.

THE WORLDXCHANGE COMMUNICATIONS FAMILY OF COM-
panies specialises in providing voice and voice-band-data
telecommunications services to residential and commercial
customers throughout the world. With global headquarters
in San Diego, WorldxChange employs a staff of highly
trained telecommunications engineers, technicians, managers, customer service personnel, sales staff, and other

support personnel worldwide.

Since its inception in 1991, WorldxChange has steadily earned an increasing share of the telecommunications market in countries across four continents. WorldxChange entered the Australian telecommunications marketplace when it opened an office in Sydney in 1995, and was poised for success when the Australian government deregulated the industry in 1997.

In Australia, WorldxChange employs more than 200 people and provides customer support services 24 hours a day. In addition to a large residential customer base, the company has targeted a cross-section of Australian businesses, including primary industry, travel, high technology, banking and finance, importers and exporters, manufacturing, and wholesale.

WorldxChange has experienced dramatic growth in its share of the highly competitive telecommunications industry in Australia. Its strategy for success includes exceptional customer service, offering subscribers

economically low call rates and using the latest, cutting-edge telecommunications technology. Business agility and the ability to respond quickly to customer and market demands for products and services continue to give WorldxChange a winning edge over its competitors.

In addition to its established operations in the United States and Australia, WorldxChange also has subsidiaries located in Belgium, Canada, El Salvador, France, Germany,

Guatemala, Mexico, the Netherlands, and the United Kingdom, to name a few, as well as an international affiliate in New Zealand. The company has developed strong business relationships with key industry providers, including most US long-distance carriers and many international carriers.

Australian Success

WorldxChange's headquarters in Sydney gives the company the advantage of being located in the hub

WORLDXCHANGE'S HEADQUARTERS IN SYDNEY GIVES THE COMPANY THE ADVANTAGE OF BEING LOCATED IN THE HUB OF AUSTRALIAN CORPORATE BUSINESS, AS WELL AS GIVING IT A PRESENCE IN A MAJOR AUSTRALIAN MARKETPLACE FOR ITS SERVICES AND PRODUCTS.

of Australian corporate business, as well as giving it a presence in a major Australian marketplace for its services and products. An audit of 12,000 privately owned businesses in New South Wales by Coopers & Lybrand revealed that WorldxChange had a gross revenue growth of more than 330 per cent over the previous year, and WorldxChange won the 1998 *Business Sydney* Growth Company of the Year award. The company's success in the Australian corporate market has also contributed significantly to the success of WorldxChange as a whole.

WorldxChange owes much of its success in Australia to its founding CEO, Richard Vincent. In the beginning, Vincent practically ran the business out of the back of his Volvo. He established the contacts to set up the technological base of the network, and then began marketing the products and services of the company.

Under Vincent's management, the company has grown rapidly, and the number of WorldxChange offices has increased as part of the plan to build a presence throughout the continent. Since 1995, WorldxChange has, on average, opened up a new switch every month around Australia.

"It is our intention to continue investment in switches over the next few years, until we cover the majority of Australia. We are now gearing to enter new markets that have been less than best addressed in the past," says Vincent.

Beyond making a contribution to the business and economic life of Sydney and Australia, WorldxChange has contributed to the development of Australia's telecommunications infrastructure. The company has a continuing commitment to research and development in the telecommunications field, and is proud of its accomplishment in enhancing Australia's telecommunications industry.

The Australian operation is the company's most successful international subsidiary outside the company's global headquarters. Roger Abbott, who founded and continues to own and operate the business, is a skilled negotiator who has steered the company's global growth. His strategy of buying fibre-optic capacity and joining consortiums has ensured that profit margins increase

while call costs to customers decrease. Today, WorldxChange has an increasing international presence, offering millions of customers cost-effective telecommunications services.

Customer Service

WorldxChange is committed to providing the highest-quality customer service to all its customers by maintaining a personal approach. The company's customer base is split equally between the corporate and residential sector, and its clients range from large airline operators to companies in the banking and finance industries to corner store operations.

The ambition of WorldxChange is to do more than offer its customers cheaper national and international telephone call charges. An innovation embraced enthusiastically by the corporate customer is the international prepaid calling card. Other services include MobilexChange and an international 1-800 service for

use in 19 countries. WorldxChange advises clients on the best mix of products for the most cost-efficient and effective communications result.

Under the guidance of Vincent, WorldxChange is looking to increase its coverage until it is Australia-wide. "The company is keen to continue developing relationships with local communities. We are confident they will like our service, particularly when they see how much can be saved when calling around the country or overseas," Vincent says.

WorldxChange extends its good corporate citizenship to supporting charities and sponsoring the arts. Beneficiaries include the Sydney Theatre Company, the Australian Museum, and the MS Society's Sydney to Gong bike ride.

WorldxChange's strategy of attracting consumers with price-competitive, world-class telecommunications products, and professional, top-notch customer service will ensure its continuing success.

Aon's name atop its Australian headquarters stands out brightly on the Sydney skyline—an appropriate symbol of the successful Australian operation, which is considered a jewel in the crown of the internationally renowned risk consultancy and insurance broking company. In an ever changing and increasingly complex world, businesses, individuals, and professional practitioners need more than the

One of the largest insurance brokerage companies in the world, Aon secured its leadership in developing services that identify and minimise risk through the establishment of specialist divisions, such as Aon Risk Services Australia Limited.

traditional services from their insurance companies. An important need is managing risk arising from legal, statutory, operational, financial, or treasury exposure, among others. Controlling risk that affects any business, individual, or professional practitioner of any size differentiates Aon and has helped significantly to propel the company's extraordinary growth.

Patrick G. Ryan—Aon's founder, chairman, and chief executive officer—foresaw the need for a provider of integrated risk consultancy, risk management, and insurance services. Ryan set about creating a company that would meet that need by refashioning his insurance broking concern. In order to provide comprehensive services that accommodate clients' preferences for personal service, he coined the management strategy "We think big but manage small".

Aon's proactive philosophy has seen it develop strengths to provide service that identifies, manages, and minimises risk, before offering traditional insurance services. When a client has a good risk-control program in place, savings on insurance costs can accrue. While some of these capabilities have been developed to meet the needs of major clients, Aon is structured in such a way that small businesses and individuals can also benefit. Aon's interdependent consultancy practices provide clients access to all its services in the broadest context of risk management.

Since the early 1980s, when it began to develop its risk consultancy operation, Aon has acquired more than 60 companies. Each of them has brought a unique perspective and expertise—as well as new skills, staff, and an additional client base—to the Aon family. According to Ryan, Aon invests in companies that enable it to bring greater value to its clients. "We are always interested in niche specialists that complement our already strong businesses by adding new capabilities or by augmenting our geographic presence," says Ryan. Today, Aon is one of the largest insurance brokerage companies in the world, with annual revenues of more than US$6 billion.

Sydney Jewel

Aon secured its leadership in developing services that identify and minimise risk through the establishment of specialist divisions, such as Aon Risk Services Australia Limited. The Aon name was introduced in Australia with the opening of the Sydney office in 1996, although Aon previously had a presence in Australia through other companies it had acquired.

The Sydney office is the Australian headquarters, and is responsible for the business in New Zealand and the Pacific Islands. There are more than 40 offices located throughout Australia in every state and territory. Of the company's 1,000 staff members in Australia, 500 work in Aon's impressive headquarters overlooking the Sydney Harbour Bridge.

The Australian operation is distinguished by having a number of

senior staff members who sit on the company's international committees. Pooling its staff's in-depth knowledge contributes to Aon's unique matrix structure, which underpins the success of the international operation. Maintaining high returns for shareholders is a driving force at Aon, and the Sydney-led operation contributes successfully to the international company's bottom line.

As a major international trading and commercial centre, Sydney is home to many international companies. The Aon office is perfectly located to act as an adviser for the internal and external operations of international companies, apart from key local Australian companies. It also services a number of Aon's most important and prestigious international accounts.

History

Originally founded in 1964 as Ryan Insurance Group, the Aon name came into being in 1987, when shareholders approved the change. Ryan Insurance Group pioneered the sale of life insurance services and extended warranties through car dealerships. Ryan's friendly and honest manner earned him a favourable reputation that helped his business quickly succeed.

In 1982, a major development in the history of Ryan Insurance occurred when it merged with Combined International Corporation. During that same year, the company developed its brokerage and consultancy business through the acquisition of major US broker Rollins Burdick Hunter.

Ryan expanded the company by continuing to acquire specialist

Aon's Australian Headquarters, Sydney

As Aon's Australian headquarters, the Sydney office is responsible for the company's business in New Zealand and the Pacific Islands. The impressive tower overlooks the Sydney Harbour Bridge

concerns in insurance. Aon became a major global broker in 1991 when it acquired Hudig Langeveldt, the largest independent broker in continental Europe. With this established European insurance identity in its embrace, Aon added the expertise of a company whose history dates back to 1680.

Significant acquisitions that Aon has added to its family include Frank B. Hall, the UK broker Bain Hogg Group, Alexander & Alexander Services Inc., and the Minet Group. Today, Aon's 40,000 employees work in more than 600 offices in some 115 countries. Its international headquarters is located in Chicago.

Matrix Structure

Aon has structured its activities to give its clients creative, cost-effective

ALBURY			LISMORE
BALLINA			MACKAY
BATHURST			MOREE
CAIRNS			MURWILLUMBAH
COWRA	**ADELAIDE**	**HOBART**	NARRABRI
DUBBO	**BRISBANE**	**MELBOURNE**	NEWCASTLE
ESPERANCE	**CANBERRA**	**PERTH**	ORANGE
FORBES	**DARWIN**	**SYDNEY**	PARKES
GLEN INNES			PARRAMATTA
GOLD COAST			ROCKHAMPTON
GRIFFITH			SUNSHINE COAST
GUNNEDAH			TAMWORTH
HERVEY BAY			TOOWOOMBA
INVERELL			TOWNSVILLE
LAUNCESTON			WAGGA

AON HAS MORE THAN 40 OFFICES LOCATED THROUGHOUT AUSTRALIA IN EVERY STATE AND TERRITORY.

solutions to minimise risk and fill their insurance needs. Aon can provide any service that a client requires from its divisions in an interdependent way.

The company's structure is shaped by the philosophy of its founder. Says Ryan, "In all of the more than 100 countries where we operate, our culture is defined by interdependence—sharing knowledge, skills, and resources among all our people. Our name, Aon, a word derived from Gaelic meaning 'unity', captures the essence of our culture." This interdependence in essence means that by design, Aon operates as a group of small businesses, and the Australian operation

reflects that design. Responsibilities for delivering services crisscross the geographical and expertise bases. Under this matrix management system, state directors have authority for activity in their region, and the specialist divisions have responsibility for delivering their expert services. In this way, a team comprising the necessary expertise is developed for each client.

Typically, a client will have a relationship with one part of the business. The challenge for Aon is to ensure that all other divisions provide a comprehensive, complementary package of services for that client. In this way, the Aon business grows, and the clients benefit from

minimum risk exposure and cost-effective insurance.

Australian Services

Aon is represented in Australia by eight companies providing insurance broking, employee benefit and risk management consulting, reinsurance, and underwriting services. Of these, Aon Risk Services is by far the biggest part of the local group, with around 1,000 employees providing insurance broking and risk management advice to the full range of clients from large corporations to individuals.

Aon Consulting provides actuarial and consulting advice on employee benefits. Aon Re provides reinsurance broking and consulting

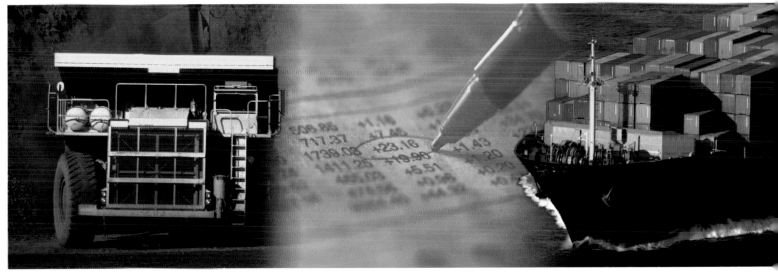

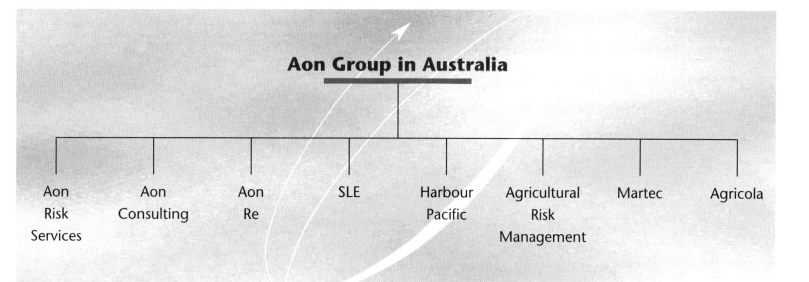

Aon Group in Australia

- Aon Risk Services
- Aon Consulting
- Aon Re
- SLE
- Harbour Pacific
- Agricultural Risk Management
- Martec
- Agricola

advice with its associate company Aon Quantix providing risk financing insurance solutions.

SLE is a specialist underwriting company with coverages for sports, leisure, and entertainment risks. Harbour Pacific has been established to provide an efficient means of writing specialist insurance products, including motor car hire.

Agricultural Risk Management is the world's leading specialist company in the assessment and management of agricultural, horticultural, and forestry risks. Martec provides consulting services specialising in the affairs of the motor industry, including quality assurance programmes for dealers, dealer performance reviews, automotive seminars, and training for sales people. Agricola is a managing underwriting agency specialising in providing insurance products to the agricultural and forestry sectors in Australia and New Zealand.

Personnel

Besides being innovative in its products and their development, Aon is distinguished by the calibre of its personnel. Many have come into the Aon fold through acquisitions made specifically to harness their intellectual capital. In the late 1980s, the Aon reputation and the changing nature of the insurance business attracted an increasing number of employees from many diverse areas, including lawyers, accountants, engineers, and environmental scientists. Aon's proactive culture demands that the company be ready with requisite expert advice when required. Niche specialists will be increasingly important as clients seek input available only from highly specialised experts.

The changing nature of the insurance industry also brings a change in the orientation of people who come to work for Aon. Candidates are university graduates with a broad education and potential for developing a unique expertise. They have excellent communication skills, and they generally view the industry in terms of providing a service for people rather than crunching numbers.

Aon supports its staff with a diverse and continuous program of training. New staff are inducted into a culture that encourages employees to be proactive, ask questions, and seek to understand developments in society and business, as well as their clients' positions in the global marketplace. Training, which is provided in-house and through external providers, covers routine procedures such as telephone answering and business writing. Aon personnel are trained to provide the same high level of service to all clients throughout the world. It is this attention to detail and service that ensures Aon will continue to grow while never compromising its personal approach in attending to its clients' needs around the world.

The Grace Hotel

SINCE ITS OPENING IN 1997, THE GRACE HOTEL HAS SEEN extraordinary success. The hotel has achieved a room occupancy rate better than that of hotels that have been operating for decades, and surpassed its own expectations in gaining market share over such a short period of time. Although the hotel is new, its spirit is reminiscent of a bygone era of luxury and style. The hotel is

LOCATED ON A SITE BOUNDED BY THREE MAJOR STREETS—CLARENCE, KING, AND YORK—THE GRACE HOTEL IS SITUATED A STROLL AWAY FROM THE BUSINESS HEART OF SYDNEY, AND IS CLOSE TO MANY OF ITS CULTURAL INSTITUTIONS AND TOURIST HIGHLIGHTS (LEFT).

THE GRACE HOTEL IS HOUSED IN THE GRACE BUILDING, A MAJOR SYDNEY LANDMARK THAT RECALLS MANY HIGHLIGHTS OF THE BUSINESS HISTORY OF THE CITY. TODAY, THE RESTORED BUILDING IS ON THE AUSTRALIAN NATIONAL HERITAGE LIST (RIGHT).

housed in the Grace Building, a major Sydney landmark that recalls many highlights of the business history of the city. Albert and Joseph Grace, who founded the Grace Brothers retail empire, purchased the building's site in 1926. The Graces employed leading architects to design the building not only to be a major architectural achievement on its own, but to set the standards for retail and office development in Sydney. Using a design based on the US Chicago Tribune Building, the Art Deco-style Grace Building was officially opened in 1930 to high acclaim.

The Grace Building served many functions over the years. In 1942, the building was requisitioned for use as the headquarters of General Douglas MacArthur, the Supreme Commander of Allied forces in the southwest Pacific during World War II. The Australian Federal Government compulsorily acquired the building in 1945 and used it to house various government departments.

The Low Yat Group, a Malaysian-based international property and hotel development company, purchased the building in 1995. Despite a strong body of opinion suggesting refurbishment as an office block, the owner, Tan Sri Dato Low Yow Chuan, saw the opportunity to transform the Grace Building into a hotel. Today, the restored building is on the Australian National Heritage list. Located on a site bounded by three major streets—Clarence, King, and York—the Grace Hotel is situated a stroll away from the business heart of Sydney, and is close to many of its cultural institutions and tourist highlights.

Four-Star-Plus Amenities

One of the many features that set the Grace Hotel apart—and the one most often praised by guests—is the size of its rooms. The four-and-a-half-star Grace Hotel contains 382 guest rooms, the smallest of which are still larger than the average-size rooms of many hotels. The rooms feature beds with specially selected mattresses, feather down pillows, and doonas—so comfortable that a high percentage of the hotel's guests praise them as the most comfortable bed they have slept in. Even so, the Grace Hotel offers competitive rates in the mid-range bracket.

Another feature of the hotel is its high level of service, and high-technology management and information services have been employed throughout the hotel to ensure that constant and consistent services are maintained. The Grace Hotel offers accurate and speedy room service, guaranteed 24 hours a day; smoke-free floors; an ice-making machine on each floor; in-room entertainment centres, complete with cable television and in-house movies; and electronic door-locking systems. For health-conscious guests, a modern, contemporary-style private gym with state-of-the-art equipment and an indoor lap pool is located on the 11th floor.

The Grace Hotel also offers several dining options. The Grace Brasserie is the hotel's à la carte and buffet restaurant, with a menu that includes Asian-inspired Australian cuisine. The Grace Deli, on the ground floor, is an informal cafe offering a friendly atmosphere for light meals and casual meetings.

CLOCKWISE FROM TOP LEFT:
THE GRACE HOTEL CONTAINS 382
GUEST ROOMS, THE SMALLEST OF WHICH
ARE STILL LARGER THAN THE AVERAGE-
SIZE ROOMS OF MANY HOTELS.

THE GRACE DELI, ON THE GROUND
FLOOR, IS AN INFORMAL CAFE OFFER-
ING A FRIENDLY ATMOSPHERE FOR
LIGHT MEALS AND CASUAL MEETINGS.

FOR HEALTH-CONSCIOUS GUESTS,
A MODERN, CONTEMPORARY-STYLE
PRIVATE GYM WITH STATE-OF-THE-ART
EQUIPMENT AND AN INDOOR LAP POOL
IS LOCATED ON THE IITH FLOOR.

THE GRACE HOTEL CAN ACCOMMO-
DATE EVENTS—SUCH AS CONFERENCES,
MEETINGS, AND PRESENTATIONS—
RANGING IN ATTENDANCE FROM 30
TO 500 GUESTS.

The Grace Wine Bar features light pasta dishes. Whatever the restaurant choice, guests will find a complete selection of Australian wines to choose from.

Corporate Guests

Tan Sri Low's vision for the hotel was to achieve an unsurpassed level of technological assistance for corporate travellers. The Grace Hotel has realised this vision by providing corporate travellers with the highest level of information technology to enhance their productivity under tight schedules. Every room has three telephones and a large, ergonomically designed workstation with adjacent data ports for fax machines, laptops, and other communication equipment. Voice mail and Internet facilities are also on hand. Security

for sensitive material is afforded by in-room safes.

Business centres in the hotel are fitted with any business tool that the corporate guest may need to conduct business. Staff are available to help with the equipment or to offer secretarial support. The Grace Hotel can accommodate events— such as conferences, meetings, and presentations—ranging in attendance from 30 to 500 guests. Specially trained staff can assist in organising any function.

Location Sensation

The hotel's slogan is The Location Sensation, and its location makes it the ideal accommodation for the leisure traveller. The hotel is within a short stroll of several shopping complexes, including the prestigious

Queen Victoria Building and the Pitt Street Mall. Also within walking distance is Darling Harbour, with its entertainment venues, including the Sydney Aquarium and the Australian National Maritime Museum. Only minutes away, Chinatown, the Sydney Opera House, the State Library, and the Parliament House are just a few of the Sydney visitor.

Tan Sri Low's visionary transformation of the Grace Building into the Grace Hotel was an innovative venture that enlivened a Sydney architectural and historical landmark. With its unique building, central location, and highly qualified staff with many years of experience, the Grace Hotel offers a unique Sydney experience for the business or leisure traveller.

BEGINNING AS A SMALL PUBLISHER OF LOCAL NEWSPAPERS in the 1930s, Towery Publishing, Inc. today produces a wide range of community-oriented materials, including books (Urban Tapestry Series), business directories, magazines, and Internet publications. Building on its long heritage of excellence, the company has become global in scope, with cities from San Diego to Sydney represented by Towery products.

In all its endeavours, this Memphis-based company strives to be synonymous with service, utility, and quality.

A Diversity of Community-Based Products

Over the years, Towery has become the largest producer of published materials for North American chambers of commerce. From membership directories that enhance business-to-business communication to visitor and relocation guides tailored to reflect the unique qualities of the communities they cover, the company's chamber-oriented materials offer comprehensive information on dozens of topics, including housing, education, leisure activities, health care, and local government.

In 1998, the company acquired Cincinnati-based Target Marketing, an established provider of detailed city street maps to more than 300 chambers of commerce throughout the United States and Canada. Now a division of Towery, Target offers full-colour maps that include local landmarks and points of interest, such as parks, shopping centres, golf courses, schools, industrial parks, city and county limits, subdivision names, public buildings, and even block numbers on most streets.

The Urban Tapestry Series

In 1990, Towery launched the Urban Tapestry Series, an award-winning collection of oversized, hardbound photojournals detailing the people, history, culture, environment, and commerce of various metropolitan areas. These coffee-table books highlight a community through three basic elements: an introductory essay by a noted local individual, an exquisite collection of four-colour photographs, and profiles of the companies and organisations that animate the area's business life.

To date, more than 80 Urban Tapestry Series editions have been published in cities around the world, from New York to Vancouver to Sydney. Authors of the books' introductory essays include former US President Gerald Ford (Grand Rapids), former Alberta Premier Peter Lougheed (Calgary), CBS anchor Dan Rather (Austin), ABC anchor Hugh Downs (Phoenix), best-selling mystery author Robert B. Parker (Boston), American Movie Classics host Nick Clooney (Cincinnati), Senator Richard Lugar (Indianapolis), and Challenger Center founder June Scobee Rodgers (Chattanooga).

To maintain hands-on quality in all of its periodicals and books, Towery has long used the latest production methods available. The company was the first production environment in the United States to combine desktop publishing with colour separations and image scanning to produce finished film suitable for burning plates for four-colour printing. Today, Towery relies on state-of-the-art digital prepress services to produce more than 8,000 pages each year, containing well over 30,000 high-quality colour images.

STEVE DAVIS

TOWERY PUBLISHING PRESIDENT AND CEO J. ROBERT TOWERY HAS EXPANDED THE BUSINESS HIS PARENTS STARTED IN THE 1930S TO INCLUDE A GROWING ARRAY OF TRADITIONAL AND ELECTRONIC PUBLISHED MATERIALS, AS WELL AS INTERNET AND MULTIMEDIA SERVICES, THAT ARE MARKETED LOCALLY, NATIONALLY, AND INTERNATIONALLY.

▶ JONATHAN POSTAL

An Internet Pioneer

By combining its longstanding expertise in community-oriented published materials with advanced production capabilities, a global sales force, and extensive data management expertise, Towery has emerged as a significant provider of Internet-based city information. In keeping with its overall focus on community resources, the company's Internet efforts represent a natural step in the evolution of the business.

The primary product lines within Towery's Internet division are its introCity™ sites, which introduce newcomers, visitors, and long-time residents to every facet of a particular community, while simultaneously placing the local chamber of commerce at the forefront of the city's Internet activity. The sites include newcomer information; calendars; photos; citywide business listings with everything from nightlife to shopping to family fun; and online maps pinpointing the exact location of businesses, schools, attractions, and much more.

Decades of Publishing Expertise

In 1972, current President and CEO J. Robert Towery succeeded his parents in managing the printing and publishing business they had founded nearly four decades earlier. Soon thereafter, he expanded the scope of the company's published materials to include *Memphis* magazine and other successful regional and national publications. In 1985, after selling its locally focused assets, Towery began the trajectory on which it continues today, creating community-oriented materials that are often produced in conjunction with chambers of commerce and other business organisations.

Despite the decades of change, Towery himself follows a long-standing family philosophy of unmatched service and unflinching quality. That approach extends throughout the entire organisation to include more than 130 employees at the Memphis headquarters, another 60 located in Northern Kentucky outside Cincinnati, and more than 50 sales, marketing, and editorial staff travelling to and working in a growing list of client cities. All of Towery's products, and more information about the company, are featured on the Internet at www.towery.com.

In summing up his company's steady growth, Towery restates the essential formula that has driven the business since its first pages were published: "The creative energies of our staff drive us toward innovation and invention. Our people make the highest possible demands on themselves, so I know that our future is secure if the ingredients for success remain a focus on service and quality."

TOWERY PUBLISHING WAS THE FIRST PRODUCTION ENVIRONMENT IN THE UNITED STATES TO COMBINE DESKTOP PUBLISHING WITH COLOUR SEPARATIONS AND IMAGE SCANNING TO PRODUCE FINISHED FILM SUITABLE FOR BURNING PLATES FOR FOUR-COLOUR PRINTING. TODAY, THE COMPANY'S STATE-OF-THE-ART NETWORK OF MACINTOSH AND WINDOWS WORKSTATIONS ALLOWS IT TO PRODUCE MORE THAN 8,000 PAGES EACH YEAR, CONTAINING WELL OVER 30,000 HIGH-QUALITY COLOUR IMAGES (TOP).

THE TOWERY FAMILY'S PUBLISHING ROOTS CAN BE TRACED TO 1935, WHEN R.W. TOWERY (FAR LEFT) BEGAN PRODUCING A SERIES OF COMMUNITY HISTORIES IN TENNESSEE, MISSISSIPPI, AND TEXAS. THROUGHOUT THE COMPANY'S HISTORY, THE FOUNDING FAMILY HAS CONSISTENTLY EXHIBITED A COMMITMENT TO CLARITY, PRECISION, INNOVATION, AND VISION (BOTTOM).

MICHAEL AMENDOLIA spent his first 15 years in photography with News Limited newspapers, followed by four years with the *Australian*. In 1987, he won Press Photographer of the Year. Currently, Amendolia is a freelance photographer specialising in documentary photography and portraiture for clients such as *Time*, *Marie Claire*, the *Australian*, *Stern* (Germany), and the *London Times*.

JASON BUSCH earned his bachelor of arts degree in photography at Victorian College of the Arts in 1989. He moved to Sydney the following year to work with Wildlight, largely in the editorial market, with clients such as the *Business Review Weekly*, *Who*, and *Australian Geographic*. Busch has worked in South-East Asia and New Zealand, where he freelanced for *North & South Magazine*, the *Press*, and the *Sunday Star-Times*. He has contributed to a number of books, including *Commemorating the Second World War*,

Wildlight Images of Australia, and *Wildlight-Sydney*.

PETER CARRETTE was born in London and began his career in Fleet Street at the age of 17 as the Frank Packer's copy boy. He came to Australia in 1966 to work as a staff photographer for Packer's magazine *Everybodys*, Australia's first rock-and-roll/show business colour publication. For the past 24 years, Carrette has worked as a freelance photojournalist, and his pictures have appeared in publications all around the world, including *Time*, *Life*, *Vanity Fair*, *Newsweek*, *Rolling Stone*, *Paris Match*, *People Weekly Magazine*, *London Daily Mail*, and *New York Times*. He has photographed the Paris collections, royal tours, and production stills on hit movies such as the *Crocodile Dundee* series and Francis Ford Coppola's war epic *Apocalypse Now*.

CLAVER CARROLL has been a photographer for 38 years and has won numerous awards, including an international Kodak competition. Assignments have taken him to 34 countries where he has photographed memorable places and events such as the Sistine Chapel, Wall Street, the White House, the Atlanta Olympics, the famine in Somalia, and the royal tours of Australia. Carroll's work has

included numerous front covers and exclusives for publications such as the *Australian Women's Weekly*, *Woman's Day*, *New Idea*, *TV Week*, major metropolitan newspapers, trade business and airline magazines, and calendars and annual reports.

MELISSA COOK studied photography in Florence, Italy, at the Santa Reparta Graphic Art Centre, as well as at the Fachhochschule Wiesbaden in Germany. She received a bachelor of arts degree in design from the University of Technology in Sydney. Cook currently freelances for photographic studios and private and commercial clientele, and her work is regularly on exhibition in contemporary galleries.

JAMES DANKS has been residing in Sydney since the age of 15. He spent four years freelancing as a professional photographer's assistant and two years as a professional photographic printer. Danks has published *Kaia From Within*, a photographic book documenting the Rabaul volcanic disaster of 1994.

ROBERT EDWARDS was born in Deniliquin, in rural New South Wales. He began his career at Capital Television Company Limited in Canberra before studying photography and film at the South Australian School of Art. Specialising in editorial and corporate photography, Edwards has photographed for clients including the *Sydney Morning Herald*, *Australian Women's Weekly*, Qantas Airways Limited, Nine Network (Australia), and National Roads and Motorists Association (NRMA). His work has also appeared at the Adelaide Fringe Festival and at London Guildhall University.

PHILIP GOSTELOW was raised and educated in Perth, Western Australia. His portraiture and documentary work has appeared in *Australian Geographic*, the *Independent*, *Observer's Life*, *Marie Claire*, *Marco Polo*, *Figaro*, *JAL Winds*, *Asiaweek*, and Cathay Pacific's *Discovery*. Gostelow's photography has also appeared in numerous exhibitions, including the 1994 *Prague & Portraits* at Tokyo's Space Edge gallery. His current work includes documentary coverage of India's traditional street performers.

LORRIE GRAHAM was born in Windsor, New South Wales. She has worked as a staff photographer for the *London Observer*, *National Times*, *Times on Sunday*, and *Bulletin*. Graham has published three books—*Australians Today*, *On the Edge*, and *Face to Face*—and her work is regularly on exhibition at Stills Gallery in Paddington.

DAVID HANCOCK was born in Wellington, New Zealand, in 1953. He has lived in Sydney since 1978, and works as a photojournalist. Hancock specialises in editorial and corporate portraiture.

GREG HARD, a New Zealander, enjoys photographing beaches and the people who inhabit them. He has recently been specialising in virtual reality immersive environments for the World Wide Web.

BLAINE HARRINGTON III calls Colorado home when he is not travelling around the globe. For 10 weeks in the fall of 1996, he journeyed 36,000 air miles to 11 countries on photo shoots. In addition, he has contributed to a variety of magazines, including *Business Week*, *Forbes*, *Time*, *Newsweek*, *National Geographic Traveler*, and *Ski*. Harrington has worked assignments for the National Geographic Society and Time Life, and has taken cover photos for such travel guides as *Fodor's*, *Frommer's*, *Insight Guides*, and *Real Guides*. His photographs have also appeared in Towery Publishing's *Chicago: Heart and Soul of America* and *Boston: History in the Making*.

GLENN HUNT began his career working for the *Australian*. More recently, he has worked for *Business Asia*, *Good Weekend*, *Panorama: The Inflight Magazine of Ansett Australia*, and many other Australian publications. In 1998, Hunt was shortlisted for the World Press Photo Master Class in Holland.

CAROLYN JOHNS, a professional photographer since 1976, originally trained as a documentary photographer with Magnum Photographers in England and France. She has worked for a variety of prestigious publications, including *Time*; London's *Sunday Times*, *Observer*, and *Daily London Telegraph*; *National Geographic*; and *Vanity Fair*. Johns has also published several books, had six major exhibitions, and worked as a unit and specials photographer on more than 33 films and telemovies for Australian and American productions. In 1981, after returning to Australia from London, she was a founding member of the Wildlight Photo Agency, whose photographers were the first Australian photographers to be commissioned by National Geographic.

TOM KEATING was trained in photography in the Royal New Zealand Air Force. He went on to become a senior photographer involved in the technical side of aerial photography and a specialist in air-to air photography, particularly from the rear seat of jet fighters. After the air force, love of travel and curiosity about the Australian outback led Keating to a dual career in nature-based tourism and commercial photography. Over the last 10 years, he has led many trips to remote regions of Australia, photographing and developing a deep understanding of the landscape, its nature, and its inhabitants.

MARK LANG worked in Sydney as an advertising photographer for 15 years, specialising in still life. On weekends he would escape the pressures of the city to seek the solace of the Australian bush, eventually choosing to pursue landscape photography wholeheartedly, leaving the commercial advertising world behind.

JAMES LEMASS studied art in his native Ireland before moving to Cambridge, Massachusetts, in 1987. His areas of specialty include people and travel photography, and his work can be seen in publications by Aer Lingus, British Airways, and USAir, as well as the Nynex Yellow Pages. Lemass has also worked for the Massachusetts Office of Travel and Tourism, and his photographs have appeared in several other Towery publications, including *Greater Phoenix: The Desert in Bloom*; *New York: Metropolis of the American Dream*; *Orlando: The City Beautiful*; *San Diego: World-Class City*; *Treasures on Tampa Bay: Tampa, St. Petersburg, Clearwater*; and *Washington: City on a Hill*.

JON LOVE began his career in the early 1980s as an assistant for Gregory Heisler and several other well-known photographers in New York. His images have appeared in publications such as *Forbes*, *Newsweek*, *Business Week*, *New York Magazine*, *Time*, and *Life*. Over the last 10 years, Love has worked with a wide range of corporate and advertising clients for Australian and overseas companies. His photographs have been featured in numerous books, including *Sheraton Hotel*; *Power-House Museum, Beyond Black & White*, *Sydney: Australia's First City*, and the Australian Graphic Design Association award book *Design Down Under*, Issues 1-3.

WENDY McDOUGALL has been taking photographs for the past 10 years. Her images have appeared in seven solo and 13 group exhibitions, and her subjects have included such notables as Tom Jones, Bob Geldof, INXS, Barry Otto, Wendy Mathews, and Russell Crowe. McDougall curated the exhibitions *Women on Women (WOW)* and—with three other photographers—*Surreal'thing* at Stills Gallery in Sydney.

GRAHAM MONRO works across the board with advertising, corporate, and editorial clients. He is a fellow of the New Zealand Institute of Professional Photography and a master in the Australian Institute of Professional Photographers (AIPP). Monro has numerous pieces in the elite Fuji Advertising, Commercial and Magazine Photographers (ACMP) Australian Photographers' Collection. He is actively involved in the business of photography through both the AIPP and the ACMP, judging and lecturing nationally for both groups.

DAVID MOORE's work has appeared in the *Observer*, *Life*, *Look*, and *New York Times*. His photographs are in many institutional collections, including the National Gallery of Australia, Art Gallery of New South Wales, Museum of Modern Art in New York, La Bibliothèque Nationale de France, and Smithsonian Institution in Washington, D.C. A collection of Moore's images, accumulated as part of the official Australian contribution to the French Bicentenary, has been toured internationally by the Eastman Kodak Company. In 1988, he was honoured by a retrospective exhibition at the Art Gallery of New South Wales and by the publication of a two-volume monograph, *David Moore: Australian Photographer*.

FIONA MORRIS lives and works in Sydney as a freelance photographer. She has exhibited work in both New York and Sydney. Morris specialises in photojournalism and the documentation of everyday life.

SANDY NICHOLSON is a professional photographer currently based in Sydney. He earned a bachelor's degree in photography from the University of Technology in Sydney. In 1996, Nicholson was voted Photographer of the Year by the Melbourne Art Directors Club. His images have appeared in *Good Weekend*, *Rolling Stone*, *Australian Style*, *Vogue Australia*, and *Panorama: The Inflight Magazine of Ansett Australia*.

NOLEN OAYDA, born and raised in Sydney, was a competitive freestyle skier until a major knee injury forced him into retirement. Internationally recognized, he was the first Australian to win two European Cup skiing awards. Still based in the Snowy Mountains, Oayda specialises in outdoor action photography with an emphasis on snow photography. With images featured in more than 50 publications worldwide, he works for clients ranging from the New South Wales and Australian tourism boards to outdoor clothing companies and an array of editorial publications.

PHILIP QUIRK is a founding member of Wildlight Photo Agency, specialising in reportage, magazine, book, and corporate assignments. His photographs have appeared in Australian publications such as the *Australian*, *Sydney Morning Herald*, *Good Weekend*, *Independent Monthly*, and *Australian Way*, and international publications including *Travel & Leisure*, the *New York Times*, and *National Geographic*. Quirk is a regular exhibitor of his personal images, and is represented in many public collections, including the National Gallery of Australia, in Canberra; Art Gallery of New South Wales; Queensland Art Gallery; and South Australian Art Gallery.

ANDREW RANKIN, originally from Melbourne, studied at the Melbourne Photography College and later at the National Gallery School in Melbourne. He moved to Sydney in 1987 to take up a full-time position with the *Sydney Morning Herald*. Since 1992, Rankin has been freelancing for the editorial/corporate market in Australia and overseas. His work can be found in the ACMP collection, and he has won AIPP awards in New South Wales and nationally.

JIM RICE has been a professional photographer for 16 years, visiting more than 50 countries before settling in Sydney. He attended Bournemouth College of Art and Design, and his images have appeared in numerous publications internationally. Rice enjoys photographing ships and the sea.

GILBERT ROSSI began his career in fashion photography, but has subsequently switched to sport photography due to his interest in competitive cycling. In 1988, he covered the XXIV Olympic Games. Rossi's client list includes *Sports Illustrated*, *Newsweek*, *Time*, and *Cosmopolitan*.

ANDREW STEPHENSON has a visual arts degree from the University of Sydney. He works independently as a commercial photographer, but is also associated with Wildlight Photo Agency. In addition, Stephenson has exhibited at the Australian Centre for Photography. He has

© WILDLIGHT / DAVID MOORE

plans for two books that he hopes to have published within the next few years.

LIZ THOMPSON has worked as a photographer and journalist in the Asia-Pacific region for the last 12 years. Her work has appeared in Australian and international publications. Thompson has written and provided photography for eight books, including the series *Fighting for Survival*, which explores the experience of indigenous communities in the face of development. She also coproduced and directed an ABC/BBC documentary set in Papua, New Guinea, which was nominated for four Australian Film Institute (AFI) awards, including Best Documentary and Best Direction. Thompson has produced numerous feature-length programs for ABC Radio National.

GRENVILLE TURNER's images reflect a fascination with the physical realities of heat, light, and distance in the Australian environment, as well as the effects of these elements on its people. He has photo-graphed the high country cattlemen of the Snowy Mountains; the drought-stricken land of outback New South Wales; India and remote parts of New Guinea; anti-smuggling operations of the North Queensland customs officers; and, most recently, the Macquarie Marshes. Turner has amassed a clientele that includes *Condé Nast Traveler*, *National Geographic*, *Time*, Ogilvy & Mather Worldwide, *Esquire*, and *Australian Geographic*. His first book, *Akubra Is Australian for Hat*, was published by Simon & Schuster in 1988.

WILDLIGHT PHOTO AGENCY PTY LTD, founded in 1985, is one of Australia's premier photo agencies and stock libraries. The company represents more than 20 of Australia's best photographers and encompasses many different photographic genres. Wildlight's stock library has more than 300,000 images in both digital and transparency formats, with concentration in photographs of Australia, South-East Asia, and the Pacific. In-house photography editor **VICKI GRAY** strives to accumulate images that evoke emotional reactions.

TONY YEATES studied photography at the Mount Lawley College of Advanced Education in Perth, Western Australia. He specialises in location photography for editorial and advertising clients including *GQ*, *Tatler*, *Condé Nast Traveler*, the *Times*, the *Observer*, BHWG, *Momentum*, Australian Tourist Commission, South Australian Tourism Commission, and New Mexico Department of Tourism. Having photographed on location in Africa, Europe, and the United States, Yeates remains drawn to Australia.

Other photographers and organisations that contributed to *Sydney: World-Class Jewel* include Bob and Suzanne Clemenz; Folio, Inc.; and Greg Probst.

Profile Writers

Bob Diracca and **Teresa Lombardi** have collaborated as freelance writers since the late 1980s on articles, reviews, and profiles on diverse subjects for state and national publications. Under the pseudonym of Rob Ditessa, their work has been published in *Business Sydney*, *Inside Business Australia*, *Artist's Palette*, *Cafe Magazine*, *Australian Photography*, *Sydney Business Review*, *Australian Jewish News*, *The New Age*, *World Farming News*, *Annals*, *Aussie Post*, *The Australian Senior*, *The Catholic Weekly*, and *Cinema Papers*.

Library of Congress Cataloging-in-Publication Data

Sydney : world-class jewel / art direction by Brian Groppe.
    p.   cm. – (Urban tapestry series)
    Includes index.
    ISBN 1-881096-68-8 (alk. paper)
    1. Sydney (N.S.W.)–Civilization.   2. Sydney (N.S.W.)–Pictorial works.   3. Sydney (N.S.W.)–Economic conditions.   4. Business enterprises–Australia–Sydney (N.S.W.)   I. Series.
DU178.L39   1999
994.1'06–dc21
                                     99-029198

[Printed in Hong Kong]

Towery Publishing, Inc.
The Towery Building, 1835 Union Avenue, Memphis, TN 38104
www.towery.com

Publisher: J. Robert Towery ☞ **Executive Publisher:** Jenny McDowell ☞ **National Sales Manager:** Stephen Hung ☞ **Marketing Director:** Carol Culpepper ☞ **Project Director:** Henry Hintermeister ☞ **Executive Editor:** David B. Dawson ☞ **Managing Editor:** Lynn Conlee ☞ **Senior Editor:** Carlisle Hacker ☞ **Editor/Profile Manager:** Mary Jane Adams ☞ **Editors:** Stephen Deusner, Jana Files, Brian Johnston, Heather Ramsey ☞ **Assistant Editor:** Rebecca Green ☞ **Editorial Assistant:** Sunni Thompson ☞ **Profile Writers:** Bob Diracca, Teresa Lombardi ☞ **Caption Writer:** Sunni Thompson ☞ **Photography Editor:** Jonathan Postal ☞ **Photographic Consultant:** Wildlight Photo Agency ☞ **Photography Coordinator:** Robin Lankford ☞ **Profile Designers:** Laurie Beck, Melissa Ellis, Kelley Pratt, Ann Ward ☞ **Production Assistants:** Loretta Lane, ☞ **Production Resources Manager:** Dave Dunlap Jr. ☞ **Production Coordinator:** Brenda Pattat ☞ **Digital Color Supervisor:** Darin Ipema ☞ **Digital Color Technicians:** Amanda Bozeman, Eric Friedl, Deidre Kesler, Brent Salazar ☞ **Print Coordinator:** Beverly Timmons

© WILDLIGHT / GREG HARD

Index of Profiles